JERRY YANG

ASIAN AMERICANS
OF ACHIEVEMENT

JERRY YANG

PAUL KUPPERBERG

CHELSEA HOUSE
PUBLISHERS
An imprint of Infobase Publishing

Jerry Yang

Chelsea House
An imprint of Infobase Publishing
132 West 31st Street
New York NY 10001

Library of Congress Cataloging-in-Publication Data
Kupperberg, Paul.
Jerry Yang / Paul Kupperberg.
   p. cm. — (Asian Americans of achievement)
Includes bibliographical references and index.
ISBN 978-1-60413-569-5 (hardcover)
 1. Yang, Jerry—Juvenile literature. 2. Telecommunications engineers—
United States—Biography—Juvenile literature. 3. Businesspeople—United States—
Biography—Juvenile literature. 4. Computer programmers—United States—
Biography—Juvenile literature. 5. Webmasters—United States—Biography—
Juvenile literature. 6. Yahoo! Inc.—Juvenile literature. I. Title. II. Series.
 TK5102.56.Y36K87 2009
 338.7'6102504092—dc22   2009015018

Series design by Erika K. Arroyo
Cover design by Ben Peterson

Printed in the United States of America

Bang EJB 10 9 8 7 6 5 4 3 2 1

This book is printed on acid-free paper.

CONTENTS

Organizing
the Web

As graduate students at Stanford University in 1994, Jerry Yang and David Filo should have been working toward finishing their doctoral degrees in electrical engineering. Their studies focused on computer-aided design and how it could be used to improve and automate the production of computer chips. Before them lay the task of writing their theses—the book-length papers necessary to earn a Ph.D. They had months and months of research and hard work ahead of them. The work, however, failed to keep Yang's and Filo's interest. Both young men were bored with their studies. Much more interesting was the new World Wide Web.

"We found every single possible way of distracting ourselves from writing the thesis," Yang admitted during a 1999 interview on the *Motley Fool Radio Show*. "We played golf and played rotisserie fantasy basketball leagues, and through all that experience we were using the Internet to do a lot of our research, and not only for real research, but also for our fantasy basketball and things like that."

The Internet in 1994 was a very different world from what today's Web surfer sees. It was, as Yang and Filo had discovered, disorganized and chaotic with no easy way to navigate from one site to another or keep track of favorite and often-visited sites. To find a Web site a second time was often difficult and time-consuming.

In an interview in April 1996 with *Metroactive* magazine, Filo remembered the frustration of those early days. "We'd wander around the Net and find something interesting, and then I'd ask Jerry, 'Hey, where was that cool page we saw the other day,' and we could never remember where it was," Filo said. "I mean, it would take us hours to just get back there, to find it. So we made ourselves a hot list, mostly to keep track of little databases and categories."

Their hot lists grew so quickly that they were soon breaking them down into categories—such as Art, Business, Computers, Economy, and so on—and, when *those* became too long, they developed smaller sub-categories. Their database of Web sites was a partial answer to the chaos that Yang and Filo encountered. As engineers, they likely found this messy, unmapped landscape offensive and, because the mind of the engineer is trained to seek out simple solutions to such situations, they were naturally drawn deeper and deeper into this work over their schoolwork.

In an old trailer at Stanford that they used as an office, Yang and Filo developed Web-searching software to find and index the sites. Their plan involved visiting and categorizing as many sites as they could for their index, which they first named "Jerry's Guide to the World Wide Web." As fans of Japanese sumo wrestling, they had named their workstations after their favorite wrestlers. Yang's machine, which was home to the index, was "Akebono," while Filo's computer, which held the software that ran it all, was "Konishiki."

On a computer named "Akebono" after a famous sumo wrestler, Jerry Yang began to compile a list of his favorite Web sites in early 1994. Joining Yang in the task was David Filo, a fellow engineering graduate student at Stanford University in California. Their lists evolved into what would become the mighty Web portal Yahoo!.

Their friends in the Stanford engineering department heard about the list and asked if they could have access to it. To accommodate them, Yang put it on his computer workstation at the university in April 1994 in HTTP (HyperText Transfer Protocol) format, a computer language commonly used on the Internet. It allowed information to have hypertext links, which users only needed to click on to take them directly to the linked Web site. While we take such ease of use for granted today, it was then still a new idea.

(continues on page 12)

Other Notable Individuals

DR. AN WANG

The development of the computer and the World Wide Web required the hard work, creativity, and inspiration of countless individuals. One of the more well-known names in that distinguished roll call is Dr. An Wang, co-inventor of the magnetic pulse-transfer controlling device for computer memory, a development that was crucial to digital information technology. He also holds more than 35 related patents.

Wang was born on February 7, 1920, in Shanghai, China. He graduated from Jiao Tong University in 1940 with a degree in electrical engineering. In 1945, Wang emigrated to the United States to attend graduate school at Harvard University, earning his Ph.D. in applied physics in 1948. Wang remained at Harvard after graduation, working with Dr. Howard Aiken (1900–1973) on the design of Aiken's Mark IV, the first all-electronic computer, at Harvard's Computation Laboratory.

Building on that experience, Wang teamed up with a schoolmate from China, Dr. Way-Dong Woo, a mathematician, to develop the magnetic pulse-transfer controlling device for computer memory, which refers to the way the device's magnetic field controls the switching on and off of current in electro-mechanical systems, as in a computer. Way-Dong Woo became ill and died before the patent was issued for their creation. Because Harvard, unlike many universities, did not hold that inventions made by members of its faculty belonged to the school, Wang became the sole holder of this valuable patent, which was not granted until 1955.

After the patent was granted, Wang sold it to IBM (International Business Machines) for $500,000. Wang used the money to expand Wang Laboratories, the company he started in 1951 to develop specialty electronic devices.

Wang's other main contribution to the development of practical computing devices was the write-after-read cycle, which also contributed to the development of magnetic core memory. The write-after-read cycle, the predecessor of today's read-only memory, allowed information to be written, or stored, so that it was not continuously overwritten and erased by the information that followed it.

Wang, who believed that "success is more a function of consistent common sense than it is of genius," expanded his company, reaching $1 million in sales in 1964. Spurred by the success of Wang Laboratories' desktop and electronic calculators with digital displays (including a calculator with remote terminals for multiple and group users), the company had 1,400 employees and $27 million in sales by 1970. In the mid-1970s, Wang introduced the first commercial word processor, which was among the first desktop computers to feature a large CRT (cathode ray tube) display. Besides calculators and word processors, Wang began to make minicomputers in the early 1970s. By 1989, the company, based in Lowell, Massachusetts, employed more than 30,000 people.

An Wang used his success to give back to science and to his community. In the late 1970s, he founded the Wang Institute of Graduate Studies in Massachusetts, offering a graduate program in software engineering. He donated substantial amounts of money to the school, including the profits from his autobiography, *Lessons*. The institute closed in 1987 because of low enrollment; ownership of the campus was transferred to Boston University. In 1983, to commemorate his contributions to the restoration of the Metropolitan Theatre, a Boston landmark, the theater was renamed in his honor.

In recognition of his work toward the development of the personal computer, Wang was inducted into the National Inventors Hall of Fame in 1988. Although Wang died in 1990 and Wang Laboratories no longer exists (it was acquired by Getronics of the Netherlands in 1999), his name lives on as an innovator in his field.

(continued from page 9)

WHAT'S IN A NAME

By then, the site was called "Jerry and David's Guide to the World Wide Web." Yang had changed the name because he was "sick and tired of taking all the credit." Still, the much shier Filo was not thrilled with the top billing.

"David hated it. He hates to have his name associated with it," Yang explained in a June 1999 interview on *Big Thinkers*, a program on the cable station TechTV. "One night we locked ourselves in a room and said, 'We need to come up with something easy to remember.' We wanted to call it "yet another something' [and] looked up all the words that started with y-a. *Yahoo* stuck out. In [Jonathan Swift's 1726 satiric novel] *Gulliver's Travels*, it means somebody who is rude, a subhuman species who were rude and uncivilized. That's us."

They also decided that Yahoo was an acronym for "Yet Another Hierarchical Officious Oracle," a self-deprecating bit of humor that showed that they did not take themselves or their list too seriously. It was a distraction from studies that had become boring to them. Why not have a little fun with their hobby before buckling down to finish their theses?

Their friends who were using the site were having a bit of fun, too. Those friends told still more friends, and soon, the world outside the Stanford campus was discovering the guide. With its categories and sub-categories, the hierarchy of the site even made it simple for novices to find Web sites. "We were in a unique situation in the summer of 1994 to be able to experience that kind of grass-roots growth, fueled by a lot of interest that was not our doing, and then just sitting back to watch the access logs go up," Yang said in an interview a year later, as cited in Karen Angel's book, *Inside Yahoo!: Reinvention and the Road Ahead*. "I don't think that could happen today." With the number of users increasing, Yang and Filo thought the time had come to redesign the site to make it easier to use and more attractive to a broader audience. The list had grown too large for their personal computers to handle, so they shifted the endeavor onto the World Wide Web. They began to add special features and links and, before they knew it, their little list had exploded into one of the most popular Web sites on the Internet.

Their little distraction was growing at a phenomenal rate, with the number of users doubling every month. So many people were accessing it that the Stanford faculty began to complain that viewers of the index were clogging and crashing the university's computer network. Without even realizing how it all came about, Jerry Yang and David Filo found themselves running an Internet company.

This fledgling company would grow—quite quickly—from an online list of favorite Web sites to one of the busiest Internet portals in the world. Under its banner, Yahoo! would soon offer Internet users a powerful search engine, e-mail, chat groups and chat rooms, bulletin boards, maps and directions, help-wanted and for-sale ads, ads for homes and cars, personal ads, music, weather, shopping, sites to store photographs, and more. Not bad for two young graduate students who were just avoiding their schoolwork.

From Taipei to San Jose and Beyond

Taiwan is an island some 100 miles (161 kilometers) east of mainland China. Only 245 miles (394 kilometers) long and 89 miles (144 kilometers) wide, or smaller than the area of Delaware and Maryland combined, the island is dominated by steep mountains and is home to more than 23 million citizens.

A military defeat in 1895 forced China to give up control of Taiwan to Japan until after World War II. The Communist revolution of 1949 sent more than 2 million Chinese nationalists fleeing the new government to establish the Republic of China on the island. The Republic of China was regarded by many Western nations as the legitimate government of China until the 1970s, when recognition switched to the People's Republic of China, the Communist government on the mainland. Over the last several decades, Taiwan has developed into one of Asia's economic powerhouses, a Pacific Rim center of commerce, industry, and trade.

Jerry Yang was born on November 6, 1968, in Taipei, the capital city of Taiwan on the northern end of the island.

Besides being a major industrial center, Taipei is also home to 20 universities. Jerry's name at birth was Yang Chih-Yuan (in China, the family name comes first). His Taiwanese mother was a professor of language and drama; his father, who came from mainland China, died when Jerry was two years old, leaving his mother to raise him and his one-year-old brother by herself.

A NEW NAME AND A NEW HOME

Jerry's mother had a difficult time supporting her family in Taiwan. Jobs were not open to female professors at most universities, so when Jerry was 10 years old, the family immigrated to the United States. She also wanted to leave Taiwan because she feared the thought of her sons being drafted by the army when they came of age. The Yangs settled in San Jose, California, in the heart of the Silicon Valley, which was becoming a center of the American computer and electronics industry.

"It wasn't an easy decision for my mom," Yang said in an interview with *Fortune* magazine. "The ability to teach English wasn't exactly a skill that was in short supply in the U.S. So even though she had the language skills to get along here, she didn't have the slightest idea what she would do. She was really brave."

Chih-Yuan's first order of business was to change his name to the more American-sounding Jerry (his mother and brother followed suit, becoming Lily and Ken), while Mrs. Yang was able to find work in her field as a professor of English and drama.

As a youngster in Taiwan, Jerry had begun to read and write his native Chinese by the time he was three years old. When he arrived in the United States, he knew only one English word—*shoe*. He picked up English quickly, however, and was soon speaking and writing like a native. He excelled in school as a straight-A student. Jerry's thirst for knowledge was no surprise

(continues on page 18)

THE IMPORTANCE OF STUDY

The Taiwan in which Jerry Yang was born in 1968 is a very different place from what it is today, but even that difference is small compared with the two cultures Yang Chih-Yuan straddled when he arrived in the United States in 1978.

Yang recalled the transition from the Chinese way of life on *Becoming American: The Chinese Experience*, a program that aired on PBS in March 2003. "I do remember leaving Taiwan," Yang told host Bill Moyers. "And it feels a bit like a dream. I was just about to turn 10. I remember landing in L.A.; you have lines upon lines of people trying to get through immigration.

"Everybody had their belongings with them, you know. Black people, white people, yellow people, all coming into the country. Basically we had everything we ever owned, you know, my mom, and my brother, and me, and a few suitcases, and we didn't really understand the language.

"You know, it was very much like a scene out of a movie. It's loud, and it's noisy. And it's big. Everything is huge. And there's land everywhere and there's cars everywhere. And so that was the imagery that I remember of my first day in the United States.

"I never felt that I didn't belong. I felt like this is where I'm gonna be. I think for me, it was much more of a journey, you know. It's a journey of understanding how in this new world I could fit in."

Yang's mother brought to America the Chinese tradition of emphasis on education. A college professor herself, Mrs. Yang pushed her children to study hard. Success would require a great deal of work, but Jerry's mother prepared her children for what lay ahead, requiring them to memorize words from the dictionary every day and quizzing them to make sure they were keeping up with their studies.

Immigrant Chinese parents in the United States generally are not as indulgent as their American-born counterparts, making sure that their children kept focused on their studies—even when they were not studying. Yang remembered that even family get-togethers would turn into study sessions: "It was very competitive with even our cousins. It was just a big part of my life. I remember we would go to my uncle's house and, you know, you go swimming or go play Ping-Pong for awhile and then you would sit there and do algebra for two hours."

Somehow, the endless studying and the striving for excellence were not considered work, although Yang had to admit, "It sounds terrible, but you know, you end up learning things that you would never [have thought you were learning], but it was almost a game. It was fun rather than being a chore. Then there's the typical thing that Chinese people do when they first get here. You randomly flip to a page in the dictionary and you gotta remember five words from the dictionary and you get tested the next day."

No matter that the Yangs were living in San Jose, attending American schools, and living an American lifestyle, they were still expected to know and understand the ways of the world they came from. And, though he might be working harder than some of his American friends, Jerry knew he had it better here than he would have had back in Taiwan.

"It's not a change from Taiwan," he said, but then reconsidered his answer. "I mean, Taiwan was even worse. . . . Actually, you get to play and study rather than in Taiwan, (where) you just get to study."

(continued from page 15)

to his mother, who recalled, "Ever since he started to speak, he was always asking, 'What is this?' and 'Why?'"

"We got made fun of a lot at first. I didn't even know who the faces were on the paper money," Yang said in the *Fortune* interview. "But when we had a math quiz in school, I'd always blow everyone else away. And by our third year, my brother and I had gone from remedial English to advanced-placement English."

Jerry's curiosity carried him through San Jose's Sierramont Middle School and Piedmont Hills High School with straight As. In high school, he played on the tennis team and was elected student-body president in his senior year. Also in his final year, he took the equivalent of his freshman-year college course load. At graduation, he was the class valedictorian. Jerry earned scholarships to every college he applied to, including Cal Tech, Stanford University, and the University of California, Berkeley. He chose Stanford because it was closer to home and because he did not have to choose a major in his freshman year. As he said in the *Fortune* interview, "I thought I wanted to be an electrical engineer, which I turned out to be. But I was always curious about other things, too, and what if I got interested in history or the law?"

Yang had to work part time while in college, and one of his jobs was as a book sorter and shelver in the university library. "That's where I first learned about how systematically information was categorized," he said. In four years, Yang completed not only his bachelor of science degree in electrical engineering but also his master's degree, earning both in 1990. Yang decided to continue his education and was accepted into Stanford's doctoral program.

At Stanford, Yang was becoming friends with a fellow graduate student in electrical engineering, David Filo. Yang's first encounter in 1989 with Filo has become a Silicon Valley

Although they had met four years earlier, David Filo and Jerry Yang became close friends when they attended a six-month teaching-assistant program in Kyoto, Japan. When they returned to Stanford University, they began the hobby that would turn into Yahoo!.

legend. Filo, who is two years older, was an instructor for one of Yang's math courses. In the class, Yang received the lowest grade of his Stanford career. The two men also shared a passion for sports. In 1993, Yang and Filo participated in the same six-month teaching-assistant program in Kyoto, Japan. This academic- and cultural-exchange program gave Stanford graduate students the opportunity to study at the Stanford Center for Technology and Innovation (SCTI) in Japan. There, Yang and Filo not only cemented their friendship, but they also met fellow students and scientists from around the world, including people who would later work for Yahoo!. And it was in Japan that Yang met his future wife, another Stanford student, Akiko Yamazaki, a Costa Rican with Japanese parents. ("When we argue, Akiko says I always have the advantage because English is my second language but it's her third language," Yang joked in the *Fortune* interview.) The two married in April 1995.

GENERATING THE "GUIDE"

When Yang and Filo returned to Stanford in 1993, everyone was talking about Mosaic, the new software that allowed browsing of information on the new World Wide Web. Mosaic was created by Marc Andreessen and his team at the National Center for Supercomputing Applications at the University of Illinois. Now, a whole world of information was available

DAVID FILO

While Jerry Yang appears quiet and thoughtful in public, his partner and Yahoo! co-creator David Filo tries to stay out of the public eye altogether. Filo, whom friends describe as quiet and reserved, was born in 1966 and grew up in Moss Bluff, Louisiana, near Texas and the Gulf of Mexico. He was the second-youngest of six children and, like his future partner, a fast learner. His family lived in a communal setting, sharing a kitchen and a garden with six other families.

Filo's interest in engineering showed itself early. "I remember looking at the Erector Set catalogue and wanting the fancy pieces," he recalled in an interview in the January 1999 issue of *Wired* magazine. "The three-speed motor versus the little one we had." When he was in fifth grade, his family built a new house. Besides being fascinated with the power tools the builders used, the experience showed him how engineering played a part in something as simple as planning a living space.

"There are eight of us in the family, and the house originally was only about 1,400 square feet," Filo said in the same through a computer. The two graduate students put Mosaic to use, and soon their "Guide" to the Web was growing in popularity.

With its hypertext link-enabled ability to track the movements of its users on the Internet, the "Guide" was attracting visitors not only locally within the university, but also across the country and, increasingly, around the world. Without any advertising and strictly by word of mouth and over Internet bulletin boards and user groups, the world was learning about Yang and Filo's amazing list.

In April 1994, their list of 100 sites was receiving 1,000 hits a week. By September, it was up to 2,000 sites and 50,000 hits a *day*. Then, in October, Netscape Communications

interview. "Our bedrooms were seven by eight feet, but we each had our own. Engineering in general is about building things, solving problems. To this day there are so many problems with what we're doing at Yahoo!—things still need fixing. What motivated Jerry and me all along was really simple: You try to come up with nice solutions."

Filo received his bachelor's degree from Tulane University in New Orleans before entering graduate school at Stanford University. There he met Yang and, together, they created a "nice solution" to the problem of keeping track of their favorite Web sites. Shortly after their hobby had taken off and become a business in July 1995, the two were asked during a *BusinessWeek Online* chat how much time they spent browsing the Internet. Yang responded, "We live, breathe, sleep on the Web . . . just kidding," to which Filo added, "No, he's not."

Today, Filo remains the quiet man behind the scenes in his role as Chief Yahoo, focusing his energies on his efforts as the company's key technologist, continuing his search for "nice solutions" to the problems that still need fixing.

In the early 1990s, Marc Andreessen developed Mosaic, software that allowed for browsing on the World Wide Web. Mosaic was instrumental in helping Jerry Yang and David Filo develop their list of favorite Web sites. Andreessen would also help the two men when they needed to move Yahoo! from Stanford University's servers.

Corporation (a company cofounded by Andreessen) introduced its beta browser and added a link from its Web site to Yahoo!. "We simply wanted to make the browser easy for people to use, and Yahoo! was the best directory available at the time," said Mike Homer, vice president of marketing at Netscape.

Traffic skyrocketed with the Netscape link. Three months later, in January 1995, Yahoo!'s list of 10,000 sites was receiving one million hits a day, astonishing the list-makers and stretching the capacity of the Stanford computer network to the maximum. Yang and Filo were beginning to have serious thoughts about turning their creation into a business.

Others were having the same thoughts and, soon, venture capitalists were visiting Yang and Filo's trailer. Venture capitalists are individuals or companies that put up the money to get new businesses started in exchange for part ownership.

Yang and Filo's first order of business, however, was to find a new host for their servers. Yahoo! was crowding university business and research off its own servers, so Stanford asked them to move their Web site to a server off campus.

Andreessen, the creator of Mosaic, solved their problem with an invitation for Yahoo! to shift to Netscape's network. "We went out and bought a Silicon Graphics Inc. server for several thousand dollars, and that was what we used to run the Yahoo! directory," Netscape's Homer said.

The decision to move Yahoo! from the college campus and into the world of business, while made out of necessity, was the start of something far bigger than the two men could have ever imagined.

"Though we didn't realize it then," Yang said in 1995, "[finding a new host for Yahoo!] was fundamentally a decision to turn it commercial."

Jerry and David's list was about to turn from a fun distraction into big business.

3

Surf's Up!

While the modern programmable computer is a relatively new idea, humans have been seeking ways to automate the act of calculation with a mechanical device since they began to use counting boards and abacuses as early as 5,000 years ago. Sometime around 10 to 70 B.C., Hero of Alexandria built mechanical performers and a theater that put on a 10-minute play. The theater was operated by a complex series of ropes and drums, allowing the operator to control which parts of the machine did what at any given time. Thus, the device was programmable.

Builders of such marvels would have to wait almost 2,000 years before electricity, micro-circuitry, and chip technology evolved to the point that these same functions could be performed by the machine itself, without human intervention.

In the centuries that followed, the quest for mechanization and programmability of routine functions increased. For example, inventors developed clocks that could be programmed to take the changing lengths of daylight into account; calculators capable of crunching numbers fed to them; and textile looms that used punch cards to "program" them to weave intricate patterns automatically. (Punch cards are paper or cardboard cards with holes punched in them in different sequences to convey instructions to a machine.)

BABBAGE, COLOSSUS, AND ENIAC

British mathematician Charles Babbage (1791–1871) is credited with designing the first machine to be recognized as a computer (although in his day, the word *computer* was defined as "one who computes" and was used to describe the people who performed mathematical computations, with or without the assistance of a mechanical device). He began by conceiving of the "Difference Engine," a complex machine that would have had almost 25,000 parts, standing 8 feet (2.4 meters) high and weighing 15 tons (13,600 kilograms). The purpose of the "Difference Engine" was to create mathematical tables with computations derived by comparing the differences between numbers. Babbage also developed the "Analytical Engine"—a room-sized, steam-powered machine that could perform an array of calculating tasks, not just mathematical tables. The "Analytical Engine" was designed to be programmable through the use of punch cards, and it was intended to have a memory, saving results for later use.

Babbage never completed his "Difference Engine" or his "Analytical Engine." His ideas remained untested until his plans for "Difference Engine No. 2" were finally used to construct the device at the London Science Museum in 1991. It returned results accurate to 31 digits, compared with the standard 8-digit result of a modern pocket calculator. The museum had built Babbage's "Difference Engine" to mark the 200th anniversary of his birth.

The U.S. government was an early adaptor of punch-card technology, using it to record and process the data collected

Doron Swade cranked the Difference Engine No. 2, one of the world's earliest computer designs, at the Computer History Museum in California. Charles Babbage conceived the Difference Engine in 1849, but he was never able to build the machine. Under the direction of Swade, the London Science Museum built a version of the Difference Engine No. 2 in 1991 to mark the 200th anniversary of Babbage's birth.

in the 1890 U.S. Census. (The census is a count of American citizens made every 10 years as mandated in the Constitution.) The machines that compiled the results were designed and manufactured by engineer Herman Hollerith. His machines were a success, as the Census Bureau finished its work in one-third the time it had taken for the previous census. Hollerith went on to form the Computing Tabulating Recording

Corporation, which would later become the technology and computer giant IBM.

Computer technology continued to advance, and the 1940s saw an explosion in research and development. With World War II raging across the globe, military scientists were interested in these machines to increase their fighting efficiency; computers could instantly calculate trajectories for missile and cannon fire, break enemy codes, evaluate weather reports, operate radar installations, keep track of troop movements, and more. Several early computers began to emerge in the 1940s: Konrad Zuse's electromechanical "Z machines" used electromagnets instead of electricity and photographic film with encoded instructions instead of punch cards. The Atanasoff–Berry Computer was the first to use vacuum tubes (sealed electronic glass containers that controlled the flow of electricity). With vacuum tubes came the slow demise of exclusively mechanical computers. In Great Britain, the Colossus, completed in 1943, decoded nearly all of the Germans' secret radio transmissions. Harvard mathematician Howard Aiken developed the Mark I, a 750,000-part, 35-ton (31,750-kilogram) computer that the U.S. Navy used to improve the accuracy of its big weaponry.

The U.S. Army Ballistic Research Laboratory's ENIAC (Electronic Numerical Integrator and Computer), completed in 1946, is often referred to as the first general-purpose electronic computer. This computer, which weighed 30 tons (27,215 kilograms) and had 30,000 vacuum tubes, was 500 times faster than any existing computing machine. Still, it had some problems. The first ENIAC was not easily programmable, as it needed to be rewired to change any of its functions. The designers and engineers soon realized the advantages of a programmable machine and developed "stored program architecture," or a computer that keeps its programmed instructions and its data in read-write, random-access memory.

A U.S. soldier in 1946 operated controls in the room containing ENIAC (Electronic Numerical Integrator and Computer) at the University of Pennsylvania. ENIAC, which weighed 30 tons, is considered the first general-purpose electronic computer.

With this advance, modern computer technology as we know it was born, and the trend toward smaller, more powerful computers continued with the introduction of the silicon chip and the microprocessor (containing an entire computer's worth of circuitry on a single chip). The introduction of personal computers in the mid-1970s and their explosion in popularity beginning the following decade was unprecedented in the history of technology. As useful as people were finding personal computers to be in their lives, however, that impact would prove to be only the beginning, thanks to a scientist's simple dream in 1962 that computers could be made to communicate and share files with one another from anywhere in the world.

ARPANET

After World War II, relations between former wartime allies the United States and the Soviet Union became strained. The two countries, with opposing political ideologies, entered into what is known as the Cold War, or a war that is waged through political, economic, and other means, rather than military means.

As a result of the escalating tensions between the world's two most powerful nations, President Dwight D. Eisenhower authorized the creation of a new agency within the U.S. Department of Defense, the Advanced Research Projects Agency (ARPA). The president was acting in response to the October 4, 1957, launch by the Soviet Union of the world's first artificial satellite, *Sputnik I*. No one knew what the Russians might be planning to launch into orbit next, including satellites to spy on those below and weapons that could be dropped from space. The United States could not afford to trail the Soviet Union in technology and space exploration.

ARPA was created to be a center of technological advancement. The agency was well funded and staffed by some of the nation's best and brightest scientists and engineers, all free to focus on their particular areas of interest. For J.C.R. Licklider, that interest was in finding a way for computers to communicate with one another. Licklider was a computer scientist at the Massachusetts Institute of Technology (MIT) in Cambridge and the man chosen to head a new ARPA agency, the Information Processing Techniques Office (IPTO). Licklider envisioned a network of computers around the world, all connected in some way. He called his idea a "Galactic Network."

But Licklider's network was still just a dream. Actually coming up with the necessary hardware and software was something else. With the resources of the Department of Defense behind him, however, he was in a position to guide the research and press for the technological advances that would make his network happen.

J.C.R. LICKLIDER: MAN AND COMPUTER

Joseph Carl Robnett Licklider was born on March 11, 1915, in St. Louis, Missouri. The only child of an insurance salesman, young J.C.R., or "Lick," as he was usually called, displayed an early interest in engineering, working on old cars and building model airplanes.

Licklider majored in physics, math, and psychology and received his B.A. in 1937 from Washington University in St. Louis. He earned an M.A. in psychology in 1938, also from Washington University. In 1942, he received his Ph.D. in psychoacoustics (the study of the human perception of sound) from the University of Rochester in New York. From 1943 to 1950, Licklider was with the Psycho-Acoustic Laboratory at Harvard University. He then moved to the Massachusetts Institute of Technology (MIT) to follow his growing interest in computer technologies.

Licklider's 1960 paper on the symbiosis, or mutually beneficial connection, between man and computer led to his being credited as an early pioneer in the field of artificial intelligence (AI), or the study of creating intelligence in machines that mimics independent human thought, and cybernetics, the theory and science of communication and control in animals and machines. His work also spoke of the need for an easy-to-use interface between man and computer, foreshadowing the age of point-and-click computing by many years.

While many scientists feared artificial intelligence might one day allow computers to overtake or even supplant humanity,

Among those whose work proved pivotal in the development of the Galactic Network were MIT scientists Lawrence Roberts and Thomas Merrill. In 1965, they established the first direct connection between two computers, one in California, the other in Massachusetts. This achievement, though significant, was accomplished over a low-speed dial-up telephone line

Licklider's article made it clear that such thinking should be left to the world of science fiction: "Men will set the goals, formulate the hypotheses, determine the criteria, and perform the evaluations," he wrote. "Computing machines will do the routinizable work that must be done to prepare the way for insights and decisions in technical and scientific thinking."

He was appointed head of the Advanced Research Projects Agency's Information Processing Techniques Office in 1962. Besides the contributions of his "Man-Computer Symbiosis" paper and the theories behind the Galactic Network, Licklider is also remembered for his earlier work in the field of psychoacoustics, including a 1951 paper that became the basis for modern models of pitch perception. He later served as the director of a project at MIT that developed the forerunner of the UNIX computer operating system, and was involved in the development of the first computer time-sharing system.

Licklider retired in 1985, becoming a professor emeritus at MIT. In his lifetime, he received many honors, including the Franklin V. Taylor Award from the Society of Engineering Psychologists in 1957 and the Common Wealth Award for Science and Invention in 1990. In 1958, he served as president of the Acoustical Society of America. Licklider died in 1990—just shy of the so-called Internet bubble of the mid-1990s, which was made possible by his pioneering work.

and just barely worked, allowing the two computers to do little more than make contact. Actual communication, the exchange of data from one machine to another, was not yet possible because the telephone wires and technology that were in use were not advanced enough to send information.

HEAVY TRAFFIC

Telephones use circuit-switching technology to connect one telephone to another. A connection, or circuit, is created when one person calls another on the telephone. As long as the two telephones are in use, the circuit between them remains open and those wires cannot be used for any other call. Only when both parties hang up is the circuit broken and those wires freed up for the next call.

The problem with circuit-switching technology is that it is too slow for the amount of information a computer must send. If the wire were a narrow tube between two telephones, voice data would be single bits of information flowing in single file to fit the narrow space; the computer's data, on the other hand, flows 24-abreast and is too large for the available space.

An alternative means of sending information was needed, and for this, the scientists in the Information Processing Techniques Office turned to a theoretical information-transference technology known as packet switching, developed by Leonard Kleinrock. Packet switching broke the information down into smaller chunks, or packets of data containing fragments of the information, each addressed to a specific destination where it would be reassembled and read. Packets could travel along different lines, which meant they would not get slowed down by the limitations of the telephone lines.

Roberts and Merrill proved that computers could talk to one another; now they needed to take Kleinrock's theory to the next step and make the technology practical. By 1969, Roberts

Leonard Kleinrock posed next to the Interface Message Processor, an early computer, in March 2007 at his office at the University of California, Los Angeles. Kleinrock created the basic principles of packet switching, the technology underpinning the Internet.

and his fellow scientists had a packet-switching network set up between four computers, three in different California locations and the fourth in Utah. And, bit of information by bit of information, these computers spoke to and were understood by each other. Thus, the first ARPANET link was established.

Word spread across the academic world, and more and more computers joined the fledging network. By the following

(continues on page 36)

Between the Generations

THE HARDSHIPS OF THE PAST

Jerry Yang and his family came to the United States in the most recent wave of Asian immigration. While leaving behind everything and everyone you know to move to a foreign land is never easy, his story is far less dramatic than those of many who came before him. In Yang's case, he was accepted in his new homeland and afforded every opportunity this country has to offer. Many earlier immigrants, though, were not so fortunate; they faced hardships, discrimination, brutality, murder, and imprisonment by their own government.

In the middle of the nineteenth century, the United States saw its first large wave of immigration from Asia as many Chinese came to this country after the 1848 discovery of gold in California. Many of these prospectors were not only after gold; they also sought freedom from repressive economic dominance after Britain's victory over China in the Opium War (1839–1842).

From the start, the Chinese were subjected to discrimination. During the Gold Rush, California imposed a foreign-miner tax that was supposed to be collected from all foreign miners but was collected only from the Chinese. Those refusing to pay the tax were attacked and, in some cases, killed. When victims' families sought justice, they learned that California law did not allow Chinese immigrants to testify against whites.

When the Gold Rush faded, the Chinese found work as tradesmen, gardeners, laundry workers, domestics, and farmers. In 1865, the construction of the transcontinental railroad opened new and hazardous opportunities to Chinese workers. In the four years it took to complete the railroad, an estimated 9,000 to 12,000 Chinese worked for the Union Pacific Railroad, taking on many of the dirtiest and most dangerous jobs for little more than half of what European workers were paid. As many as 1,000 Chinese died during the project in avalanches and accidents with explosives.

At the great ceremony marking the end of the project, Chinese workers were handed one final indignity. As Helen Zia wrote in her book *Asian American Dreams: The Emergence of an American People*, "The speeches congratulated European immigrant workers for their labor but never mentioned the Chinese. Instead, Chinese men were summarily fired and forced to walk the long distance back to San Francisco—forbidden to ride on the railroad they built."

In 1882, following a wave of anti-Chinese violence that included riots, lynchings, and other murders, Congress passed the Chinese Exclusion Act. The act barred further immigration from China and prevented Chinese in the United States and their American-born children from becoming citizens. It would remain as law until 1943.

In the 1890s, Japanese workers began to come to Hawaii and the West Coast as cheaper replacements for Chinese workers. By 1907, sentiment had shifted against them, and they too were barred from American shores.

After the Japanese attack on Pearl Harbor in December 1941 drew the United States into World War II, American residents of Japanese descent became suspect in their own land. Afraid that their loyalties were to Japan rather than the United States, President Franklin Roosevelt issued Executive Order 9066, revoking the rights of Japanese Americans (two-thirds of whom were U.S. citizens). The order led to 112,000 Japanese Americans being placed into prison camps in seven states.

In 1924, immigration to the U.S. from various countries was limited to specific levels. The number of Asians allowed under the system was minimal. The 1965 Immigration and Nationality Act changed that, lifting restrictions based on national origins and creating specific guidelines based on family and economic need. From 1971 to 2002, almost 19.5 million immigrants from all over the world came to the United States—7.3 million of them were born in Asia, with Chinese immigrants ranking right behind those from the Philippines.

(continued from page 33)

year, computers at MIT, Harvard, numerous government agencies, colleges and universities, and private companies were on the ARPANET. Of course, in the early 1970s, computers were found only in such institutions; the personal computer was still a decade in the future, and only computers specifically linked to the ARPANET could access the network.

Although it remained the bastion of the few and was complicated to use, the ARPANET was unveiled at the 1972 International Computer Communications Conference. This was the public's first look at what would one day become the Internet.

Electronic mail, or e-mail, also made its debut in 1972 as a way for those on the ARPANET to "talk" with one another across the network. As with everything in the early days of the Internet, the software had to first be developed and written to accomplish a series of functions: writing, receiving, forwarding, and storing electronic messages, all in the blink of an eye.

As more users were logging on, new computer language was developed to handle the increasing traffic. These included File Transfer Protocol (FTP) and Transmission Control Protocol/Internet Protocol (TCP/IP). These protocols allowed dissimilar types of computers to share files and enabled computer users to communicate with different computer networks. These programs, developed in those early days of the Internet, are still being used today.

START YOUR SEARCH ENGINES

There were several problems caused by the growing popularity of the ARPANET, chief among them being the increasing number of Web sites and the difficulty early Web surfers had in making their way around this new cyberworld. New sites were being added all the time, but people could only go to sites they knew about. There was no way yet to see what other sites might be out there. Nor was there a way to easily search for them.

The first attempt at organizing the Internet was software called "Archie," developed in 1989 at McGill University in Montreal, Canada. Archie automatically searched, collected, and stored new Web sites as they came online, making them searchable, so a user could seek out a specific file. But the UNIX-based software was too complicated for the average Web surfer to learn easily and remained a tool of the advanced user. Other search-and-store programs, such as the Wide Area Information Server (WAIS), were also developed, but they shared Archie's difficulties.

In 1991, computer scientists at the University of Minnesota unveiled "Gopher." Easy to use even by those without specialized computer skills, Gopher was a great step forward in search-engine technology, even if it could only access the files on the university's network. Software engineers around the world, though, were soon duplicating Gopher for their own local networks, and it was only a matter of time before the next logical technological advance was made, the development of software to organize all this mass of scattered data into a searchable list.

The University of Nevada, Reno, won the race with a program called VERONICA, or Very Easy Rodent-Oriented Network Index to Computerized Archives. The developers used a piece of software they called a "spider," which acts as a search engine, roaming the Internet and following every Gopher menu it found. That local network's menu was then sent back to a central index, where it was stored to be searched by any VERONICA user.

Meanwhile, in Geneva, Switzerland, a computer scientist named Tim Berners-Lee was leading a team at the European Laboratory for Particle Physics. Berners-Lee was concerned that the scientists at the world's largest particle physics lab had no way of sharing information with one another. His solution was the creation in 1991 of what would soon be

Tim Berners-Lee, seen here in 1995, created the World Wide Web while working at the European Laboratory for Particle Physics. He developed the Web to allow people to access information from a remote computer without having to log on to that computer.

known as the World Wide Web, a way to access information from a remote computer without logging on to that computer to do so.

The World Wide Web used its own special computer language called hypertext. With hypertext, links—which were visible to users as underlined words—were imbedded directly into the text of a file. A click on a hypertext link sent the user directly to the desired Web page.

In 1993, Marc Andreessen at the National Center for Supercomputing Applications at the University of Illinois introduced Mosaic to the World Wide Web and revolutionized the Internet. Mosaic was a browser that employed a graphical user interface (GUI), allowing users to search the Web using both words and pictures.

For compulsive surfers and list-makers like Jerry Yang and David Filo, Mosaic was a revelation. For the rest of us, it was the dawn of a whole new age.

Riding the Wave

The World Wide Web was born out of a political and scientific need, but it quickly grew into something beyond anyone's expectations. The explosive growth of the personal computer in the 1990s—and, since then, of the laptop computer—made the World Wide Web easily available to everyone, not just scientists and government workers.

The Galactic Network was created to enable the sharing of information and, regardless of your interest or the subject you need to research, that information is likely available with the click of a mouse.

What no one could foresee was how quickly the Internet would evolve from an information-delivery system to a commercial portal. Online shopping, or e-commerce, was seen as a curiosity in 1996. By 2002, it was an accepted fact of life; half a decade later, online shopping was growing by double-digit leaps every year. The appeal and cost-effectiveness of online shopping, banking, and investing are obvious: They are quick, easy, and safe, and save time and

Back in 1995, when Jeff Bezos *(above)* launched Amazon as an online bookstore, e-commerce was a curiosity. Now, shopping online is commonplace, and Amazon has grown into the top Internet retailer in the country.

money by eliminating the need to travel and the cost of gasoline and parking.

At first, e-commerce was largely the province of e-businesses, or companies specifically created to do business online. Online retailers like eBay.com and Amazon.com began as the ideas of people who saw the growing power of the Internet and how it could be used in business. Some of their stories are every bit as amazing as Yahoo!'s.

Amazon.com, for example, was launched in 1995 by Jeff Bezos as an online bookstore. Bezos changed its original name, Cadabra.com, when it was pointed out how much it sounded like the word *cadaver*. The newly rechristened Amazon, named for the world's largest river, could offer customers an almost limitless number of book titles for sale, an impressive inventory that soon was supplemented by an entire mall's worth of products, from DVDs and CDs to furniture and automobiles. Today, less than 15 years since it was launched, Amazon.com is the largest online retailer in the United States; the number-two retailer is Staples.com, at nearly one-third of Amazon's sales. Amazon has seen steady growth, with revenues of $3.9 billion in 2002 increasing to $19.1 billion in 2008.

Internet service providers (ISPs) like CompuServe, Prodigy, and AOL were also growing successes as they sold access, via slow dial-up telephone lines in these pre-digital-service days, to the Internet's information and commercial sites.

YAHOO!

As the old saying goes, "Build a better mousetrap, and the world will beat a path to your door." Jerry Yang and David Filo had done just that, building an efficient, easy-to-use search engine that made sense out of the Internet's chaos. With nothing more than a brief message posted on a Usenet group for computer scientists—"We have a pretty comprehensive listing at the Yahoo! Database. It's an attempt to be organized by subject (although not very well)—but we are working on it."—and word of mouth, Yahoo! had become one of the hottest destinations on the Web by early 1995.

The partners continued to treat Yahoo! as a hobby, something with which to have fun and help their friends and fellow scientists. They gave little thought to the idea of making any money from this endeavor, much less having any expectation of ever being able to earn a living from it.

Others, with more business savvy and experience, saw Yahoo! differently.

Internet and software powerhouses like America Online, Prodigy, and Microsoft hungrily eyed Yang and Filo's creation. They made repeated offers to buy their way into Yahoo! and would have been happy with any level of involvement, from outright ownership to partnerships and collaborative efforts. By 1994, any one of these companies had more than ample resources to make the two graduate students very rich men. At the time of these offers, however, Yang and Filo were simply not interested in money. Yahoo! was still fun and a challenge. And if it was worth such sums to these business suitors at the time, it would be worth even more once they were done having their fun with it.

With their servers having moved from the Stanford University computer system to Netscape's network, Yang and Filo began to give serious thought to the business side of their operation. It was clear that they were having no trouble attracting a steady and increasing flow of satisfied and loyal users. The question was how to turn that into a business.

"David had it in his gut very early on that Yahoo! could ultimately be a consumer interface to the Web rather than simply a search engine or piece of technology," Yang said in a 2000 interview with *Fortune* magazine. "We weren't really sure you could make a business out of it, though."

If they were going to try, pursuing their Ph.D.s at the same time would be impossible, so the partners took a leave of absence from Stanford University, planning to complete their studies at some point in the future. Neither man has, and Yang recalled that this unfinished business "was really, really hard (to consider). I'm not a quitter."

Rather than quitting, though, they were actually at the start of an entirely new venture.

Yang and Filo, who had given themselves the title of Chief Yahoos, recognized their limitations as businessmen. They turned to one of Yang's old college friends for help. Tim Brady was a student at Harvard Business School, where one of his assignments was to write up a business plan for a new enterprise. Brady created a business plan that not only satisfied his class requirement but also served

SILICON VALLEY

The New York City and Washington, D.C., metropolitan areas may have more high-tech workers than the northern end of the Santa Clara Valley in California, but according to a 2008 study, this area south of San Francisco Bay, including the cities of San Jose and Sunnyvale, has the most high-tech workers per capita of any U.S. metropolitan region. More than one-quarter, or 286 out of every 1,000 jobs, are in the private-sector high-tech field—giving this area the nickname by which it is known the world over, Silicon Valley. (Silicon is the chemical element used to manufacture computer chips.)

Even before the computer age, the Santa Clara Valley had been home to the electronics industry. Lee DeForest, inventor of the vacuum tube, which made radio and television transmission possible, moved to the area in 1910. The Federal Telegraph Corporation, based in Palo Alto, California, began the first global radio communication system. The real boom, though, arrived in the 1950s.

After World War II, soldiers returning from the war flooded U.S. colleges. Frederick Terman, the dean of engineering at Stanford University in Palo Alto, proposed that the university create the Stanford Industrial Park by developing some of its vast tracts of unused land. The industrial park would provide low-cost facilities to technology companies that would, in turn, provide employment for Stanford's graduating students.

The Stanford Industrial Park's first tenant was Varian Associates, a company founded in 1931 by a Stanford graduate to build military radar components. Terman also helped new companies as an outline to run Yahoo! successfully. Brady's business plan stated that Yahoo would attract users and advertisers by adding content like news feeds, bulletin boards, and chat groups.

in the private sector find venture capital to get off the ground. In 1953, two graduates of Stanford University moved their start-up computer firm from the garage of one of the partners to the now renamed Stanford Research Park. William Hewlett and David Packard's company is now the world's largest manufacturer of personal computers.

In the decades since, the world of technology has seen a steady flow of innovation and world-changing advancement from the companies that call Silicon Valley home. The integrated circuit, the microprocessor, the microcomputer, and a host of other key developments were made thanks to companies like Intel, Fairchild Semiconductor, Shockley Semiconductor Laboratory, Eastman Kodak, General Electric, and others. Apple Computer, another company started in a garage, was made possible by the availability of venture-capitalist money, leading to its explosive 1980 $1.3 billion IPO (initial public offering, or the sale of a new company's stock to public and corporate investors). This led, in turn, to a succession of ever-larger high-tech IPOs throughout the 1980s and into the 1990s.

The term *Silicon Valley* did not exist until 1971, when Northern California businessman Ralph Vaerst coined it. It first appeared in a series of articles entitled "Silicon Valley U.S.A." that appeared in *Electronic News*, a weekly trade newspaper. Silicon Valley remains one of the top research and development centers in the world. In 2006, the *Wall Street Journal* found that 10 of the most innovative towns in the United States were in the valley, where orchards once grew, giving it the very different nickname of the Valley of Heart's Delight.

With a business plan in hand, Yang and Filo began to meet with Silicon Valley venture capitalists, the money people who could supply the financing required to transform a hobby into a business.

Despite the value of Yahoo!'s heavily trafficked site and the proprietary software that made it so successful, a few aspects of the start-up company made potential investors wary, including concerns about Yang and Filo's ability to run the business and the childish sounding name of Yahoo!. Even without those factors standing against Yahoo!, new Internet businesses were risky investments. Although some had proved wildly successful, the majority of startups failed within the first year.

Ultimately, however, Yahoo! proved too tempting to one investor, Mike Moritz of Sequoia Capital. Moritz shared concerns over the risks, but he was known in Silicon Valley for possessing a keen nose for successful start-ups, having helped launch such earlier companies as Apple Computer, Atari, Cisco Systems, and Oracle.

At the same time, America Online, then one of the largest Internet service providers, offered to buy Yahoo! outright. Had they accepted the offer, Yang and Filo would have been rich, but they would have lost control of their company. "We finally decided . . . on [venture capital] funding because we wanted to be an independent voice, and I think going with a corporate sponsorship would have tainted the site," Yang said, as cited in *Inside Yahoo!*.

"It was a suicide impulse on our part," Moritz would later joke about his investment, but in April 1995, after meeting with the enthusiastic young creators of Yahoo!, he committed $1 million to the company in exchange for one-quarter ownership. This meant that Moritz and Sequoia Capital believed Yahoo! was worth $4 million. By 1999, that share was worth $8 billion and, at its height of value in January 2000, more than $30 billion.

But there was a lot of hard work ahead before Yahoo! could even dream of such growth.

OPEN FOR BUSINESS

Philip Monego, a businessman who ran a company called Technology Perspectives in Silicon Valley, met with Yang and Filo before they accepted Moritz's money. Monego, an experienced online entrepreneur, was a user and a fan of Yahoo!. He believed the two young engineers had a powerful idea that they would be foolish to sell outright to anyone else at any price. Monego, who would lead Yahoo!'s interim management team, was excited to be involved with the new company.

"I was expecting a couple of bright college kids who were Internet junkies," Monego said in *Inside Yahoo!*. "What I discovered were two of the brightest, most visionary people I'd ever met at any age, who were committed to an ideal, which was to make the Internet more usable for everyone. Jerry, in particular, had a vision for how the Internet could change our lives. He was extraordinary in his ability to grasp the size of the Internet and how it could be complete. None of us got that large in our vision."

A company needs that vision, of course, but it also needed what Monego called in the same book "adult supervision to come in and build an organization around David and Jerry."

"Thousands of people were producing new Web sites every day," Filo said in an interview for a Stanford University School of Engineering publication. "We were just trying to take all that stuff and organize it to make it useful. As it became more popular, it became pretty clear we would have to get more people involved."

Sequoia Capital's check was deposited on April 10, 1995. That same day, Monego and Eric Hall, an experienced Silicon Valley money man brought in to be Yahoo!'s chief financial

(continues on page 50)

Other Notable Individuals

DR. WU-CHUN FENG

On February 28, 2004, the Chinese Institute of Engineers/USA honored Dr. Wu-chun Feng for his many research achievements by naming him the 2004 Asian American Engineer of the Year. At the time, Feng was leader of the Research and Development in Advanced Network Technology Team in the Computer and Computational Sciences Division at Los Alamos National Laboratory in New Mexico. The year before, Feng received the prestigious R&D 100 Award, given by *R&D Magazine* to the top 100 technological innovations of the year. The award recognized his work on a supercomputer (an extremely fast computer that can perform hundreds of millions of instructions per second) called Green Destiny, an environmentally friendly supercomputing cluster that used about one-tenth the electrical power of other comparably powered supercomputers.

Born in Ann Arbor, Michigan, in 1966, Feng received a B.S. in music and electrical and computer engineering in 1988 from Penn State University, where he also got his M.S. in engineering in 1990. He earned his Ph.D. in computer science at the University of Illinois at Urbana-Champaign in 1996.

At Los Alamos, Feng led researchers from several laboratories in an effort to push the limits of the Internet. They did this in 2003 by setting a new Internet Land Speed Record by sustaining 2.38 billion bits a second over a distance of more than 6,200 miles (9,978 kilometers) between California and Switzerland. In comparison, most digital subscriber line (DSL) cable services advertise speeds for residential use ranging from 128,000 to 300,000 bits a second.

The applications for such super-fast networks and processing speeds are endless. For example, the increase in speed allowed Feng's team to transform genome sequencing software (used in analyzing and mapping DNA) to reduce the time it took to search genome-sequencing results from 24 hours to less than 8 minutes.

Feng spent seven years at Los Alamos before moving to Virginia Polytechnic Institute and State University, known as Virginia Tech, in 2006 to direct the Systems, Networking, and Renaissance Grokking Laboratory, which is involved in research on high-performance networking and computing from hardware to applications software.

For his involvement in the development of environmentally friendly computer technology, he is known as "Mr. Green Destiny." His Green Destiny supercomputer, according to his Web page, "operated without any unscheduled downtime for its two-year lifetime while running in an 85°F (29°C) warehouse at 7,400 feet (2,256 meters) above sea level with no air conditioning, no air humidification, and no air filtration."

Feng recognizes Jerry Yang's contribution to the Internet every time he sits down at his computer. "I would say the Web browser provided the mechanism to popularize and democratize the Internet. What Jerry Yang and Yahoo! did back in 1996 was to leverage this mechanism to pioneer the notion of a 'news and information aggregator.'

"Now you see these aggregators all over the place. Furthermore, it has evolved as an aggregator in other arenas: one-stop shopping, like at Amazon.com, one-stop price comparisons such as Pricegrabber.com and Bizrate.com, and so on. And now we have things like RSS feeds to deliver, 'push,' information to us. This has helped keep us more informed, whether a scientist or not."

Though American-born, Feng understands that his Asian heritage comes with an added responsibility that recognition as Asian American Engineer of the Year underscores. Of winning the award, Feng said, "This is a tremendous honor, one that reflects upon the unwavering dedication and invaluable contributions of the talented engineers and scientists with whom I work.... I hope the recognition given to my work ... inspires young Asian Americans to explore careers in computer science and engineering."

(continued from page 47)

officer (CFO), signed a lease for Yahoo!'s first offices outside the Stanford University trailer at 110 Pioneer Way in Mountain View, California. The entire office, one corner of a building where semiconductors were once manufactured, had only 1,500 square feet (139 square meters) of space, about the size of a large two-bedroom apartment, forcing everyone to share, including executives Monego and Hall. About those early days, Hall said, "We couldn't get out of our chairs at the same time without hitting each other."

THINK CHEAP

Pioneer Way was just a step up from Yang and Filo's trailer on the Stanford campus. Offices, tiny to begin with, housed three staff members each, sharing one telephone per office. The roof leaked, and trash cans were often pressed into service to catch the water.

To save money, Yahoo! bought used or bargain-priced office furniture and found many office supplies at going-out-of-business sales. Along with Randy Haykin, who had been hired as vice president of sales and marketing, Yang, Filo, Monego, and Hall painted the new offices themselves. The company spent only $25,000 to ready and furnish its offices, knowing that Moritz's $1 million investment would have to last. As Monego recounted in *Inside Yahoo!*, "Mike was committed to put a million dollars into Yahoo! and no more. It was either going to prove itself or fail on that million."

Money was tight everywhere. The two Chief Yahoos drove cars so old and rusty that an employee accidentally poked a hole through the side of Filo's Toyota Tercel with his fist. They called on another Stanford classmate, David Shen, to design Yahoo!'s now-familiar logo of off-kilter, uneven lettering with the two Os staring like a pair of eyes, paying him $500 and Yahoo! stock for his efforts. Shen would later be hired as the company's "Gooey Yahoo," whose job it was to make the Web site look and feel friendly and inviting.

Even when it came to ways to improve service and speed on the network, the founders of the new company sometimes seemed to lose sight of the big picture over the details of money. Yahoo! was operated from 100 servers run by two hosting companies in Silicon Valley, meaning that in the event of a local power failure or disaster, the site would be knocked offline without a backup system. A proposal to correct the problem required each server to be outfitted with a second network-interface card at a cost of $50 per server. Filo was concerned about the $5,000 price tag, forgetting that it was being spent to improve the safety and security of Yahoo!'s multimillion-dollar Web site.

While Filo focused his energies and skill on the computer architecture and infrastructure, Yang turned his talents to the areas of corporate strategy and public relations. One of Yang's first calls was to Brady, who had crafted Yahoo!'s original business plan. As Yang said in *Jerry Yang and David Filo: Chief Yahoos of Yahoo!*, "It seemed like a natural move. He had all these ideas about marketing our product, so we made him director of marketing."

By now, search engines were popping up all over the Internet, but none were as well-suited for the task as Yahoo!, which offered not just a simple list of search results, but an entire system of categories and sub-categories. It was like a tree of information with branches to take users from general topics, like biology, down to specifics, like cellular reproduction. Brady knew that it was this unique function of the Yahoo! search engine that needed to be publicized.

To do this, the company chose the Niehaus Ryan Group to handle its publicity. This proved to be a good move, with

Srinija Srinivasan, a friend of Jerry Yang's and David Filo's from Stanford, was one of their first hires at Yahoo!. As chief ontologist, her job was to oversee Web-site review and categorization. Early on, everyone at Yahoo! was responsible for seeking out interesting Web sites to include on the list.

Niehaus Ryan crafting the memorable "Do you Yahoo?" advertising campaign, which featured a parade of unusual people in search of information on the Web about their even more offbeat interests.

Another old friend from Stanford whom Yang and Filo turned to was Srinija Srinivasan, an expert in artificial intelligence they knew from their six months of study in Japan. Her title was chief ontologist—an ontologist is someone who studies the nature of existence—and her job was the oversight of Web-site review and categorization. She was also in charge of the six local college students who surfed the Web for Yahoo!, seeking out interesting sites, checking links, and highlighting the best sites. Monego recalled receiving "hundreds and then thousands, then tens of thousands of requests per day" from sites wanting to be included on Yahoo!'s list. Srinivasan's surfers were not alone in these efforts; everyone on staff was expected to click through 100 to 300 Web sites a day. New links were added by the hundreds every week, sometimes as many as 1,000 a day.

Business was booming even as some began to wonder just *what* business it was that Yahoo! was in.

5

Growing Pains

Yahoo! was on its way. Employees were slowly filling the cramped offices on Pioneer Way, from Web surfers to corporate executives, and users kept coming to the Web site. Jerry Yang and David Filo suddenly had a big business on their hands and, as neither was a businessman, they knew they had to continue to find professionals to take these important jobs.

Their highest priority was to find the right person to be Yahoo!'s president and chief executive officer (CEO). On the one hand, they wanted someone with a knowledge and understanding of business. On the other, they did not want a stodgy, corporate type who could not understand the looser, free-form ways of Yahoo!.

"THE FIRST GREAT INTERNET BRAND"

This person would be important in helping shape the company's future. In preparation for the upcoming commercial launch of its new site, Yahoo! had begun to sell advertising through a company called Interactive Marketing. Advertising was a key part of the business plan but only a part—and an unproven one at that. Banner advertising, the boxes that appear at the top of Web sites, had only first appeared on Hotwired.com in October 1994. Several other Web sites had followed suit, but the experiment was too new to have yielded any definite results.

No one yet knew how effective these ads would be with users and surfers, accustomed to an Internet free of advertising. Banner ads also posed technical problems, often taking too long to load and slowing down the system. "We're putting a lot of time into making the ads unobtrusive and interesting, and trying to intelligently integrate them," Yang said in a 1995 interview cited in *Inside Yahoo!*.

The rest of the company was still a work in progress. The executive team was looking at all of its options, taking the parts of Tim Brady's original business plan that they liked and experimenting with the rest.

Yahoo! was making the Internet giant AOL nervous, and that company's vice presidents made frequent visits to Pioneer Way. But when Monego, Yang, and Filo met with AOL CEO Steve Case to discuss selling a 10 percent share of Yahoo! to AOL for $4 million, the offer was rebuffed. AOL would be building its own search engine, which, Case informed them, would likely put Yahoo! out of business.

Meanwhile, Yahoo! began to branch out toward becoming a media company, not just a directory of Web sites. John Taysom, a marketing vice president with the Reuters news service, proposed that Yahoo! feature his company's news articles on the site, enabling interested readers to delve deeper into the news by searching for relevant and related stories on Yahoo!. Taysom recalled in *Inside Yahoo!*, "When we wrote the contract, we had to stipulate that, because of our independence, they wouldn't put our content next to advertising that might be

(continues on page 58)

Other Notable Individuals

DR. RAJ REDDY

Raj Reddy has some questions about intelligence, such as: What is it? How is it used? And can it be learned . . . by a machine?

Dabbala Rajagopal "Raj" Reddy was born on June 13, 1937, in Katur, Andhra Pradesh, India. He received engineering degrees in India and Australia before earning his Ph.D. in computer science from Stanford University in 1966. Reddy was the first doctoral student to graduate at Stanford under Turing Award winner and artificial-intelligence pioneer John McCarthy. Reddy himself won the Turing Award, the highest honor in computer science, in 1994.

Reddy has been a faculty member at Carnegie Mellon University in Pittsburgh, Pennsylvania, since 1969, serving as the founding director of the Robotics Institute and the Dean of the School of Computer Science. Reddy was an assistant professor of computer science at Stanford from 1966 to 1969.

Reddy's research has centered on the perceptual and motor aspects of artificial intelligence, such as speech, language, vision and robotics, areas that have led Reddy's research team to look at how artificial intelligence will affect the field of robotics as well as computers and the World Wide Web.

For Reddy and anyone else involved in artificial-intelligence research, the barrier to break is the so-called Turing Test, first described by AI pioneer Alan Turing in 1950. To pass the test and demonstrate intelligence, a computer must be able to converse with a person without that person being able to tell he or she is talking with a machine.

Computers have been programmed to do many complex tasks, but no computer has yet been able to disguise the truth from a human. The human mind is able to respond almost instantly to unexpected situations, as well as remember and *learn* from past experiences.

In an interview in the *Pittsburgh Post-Gazette* in June 1998, Reddy explained, "When we say, 'Hi, how are you,' we don't think of that as intelligence. But that's actually the hard part." The article added, "Such intelligence involves the simple yet complex task of perception, which is a difficult concept to define, much less emulate."

While researchers might one day be able to create an artificial intelligence that can pass the Turing Test, Reddy has come up with what he calls an "80/20 rule" to deal with the problem. In the 80/20 rule, the computer or robot is made to perform the 80 percent of a task it can handle and leave the 20 percent calling for human knowledge and experience to people. "The idea is that man and machine work together interactively," Reddy said.

The hope is one day to achieve a computer system that will understand and recognize the spoken word as quickly and as accurately as a human—a project, Reddy told the *Post-Gazette*, "I'll spend the rest of my life on." But artificial intelligence is not Reddy's only area of interest, as he is also involved in a project whose goal is to put "the sum of all human knowledge" on the World Wide Web for all to use, share, and contribute to. It, too, is "what I intend to spend the rest of my life working on," Reddy said. Reddy will also be spending the "rest of my life" on yet a third project, the creation of a nationwide super-fast computer network with the federal government.

Dr. Reddy does not expect to live three lifetimes but said of his many projects, "They're all interrelated. . . . In order to solve any one of them, you have to solve all of them."

Still, the feasibility of ever achieving true artificial intelligence is a question on which Reddy remains philosophical. "There are many things, while they may not be themselves worthwhile, you learn so much getting there," he said. "Society has to find a way to fund crazy, way-out ideas. We know that many discoveries have happened through accidents."

(continued from page 55)

politically biased or had to do with alcohol. They quickly came back with a set of rules for the independence of Yahoo!. They wanted to be the Switzerland of information on the Web. They saw Reuters as a model for independence." (Switzerland has a long history of staying neutral.)

Yahoo! and Reuters struck a deal that brought both companies a large amount of revenue and gave the European-based Reuters, long the third-place news service behind Associated Press and United Press International, a higher profile in the U.S. marketplace. The first news feeds would appear in August 1995. Based on its deal with Reuters, Yahoo! was able to assemble a pilot program of six advertisers, including heavy hitters like General Motors and Visa.

Still, the founders never forgot that the users had to come first. As a businessman, Taysom understood that Yahoo! had to make money; as creators of the site, Yang and Filo were concerned that users would feel betrayed by the commercialization of Yahoo!. They were realistic enough, however, to recognize that Yahoo! was not just a directory and search engine but a brand name to be licensed and a media company to be capitalized on.

In other words, Yang and Filo were trying not to corrupt Yahoo!'s unique strengths while finding ways to make money off other aspects of the Web site. They were not alone in this belief; at a technology and media conference in San Francisco, Bob Metcalfe (the co-inventor of Ethernet and the founder of the tech company 3Com) said, after hearing Yang make a presentation about Yahoo!, "This is going to be the first great Internet brand."

This attitude explains why Yang and Filo remained skeptical about advertising. In July 1995, Yang told a *BusinessWeek Online* chat, "We are trying to have a handful of sponsors to sponsor various categories of Yahoo!, but we don't envision tons of advertising/yellow page stuff on Yahoo!. The goal is to maintain a clear separation between the 'directory' part, which is objective and is consistent with our editorial tone, and the 'commercial' part, which is clearly sponsored content."

To ensure that Yahoo! did not lose sight of the user over the advertiser, Yang and Filo decided on an approach that was summed up in their motto, "If we don't like it, we figure you won't like it."

A NEW YAHOO!

Until now, Yang and Filo had been hiring friends from Stanford and finding the help they needed to launch their new business among consultants and venture capitalists who believed in the Yahoo! mission. For CEO, however, they left the search up to a professional headhunter, or someone who matches executives with specific jobs.

Among the half-dozen leading candidates for the position was Tim Koogle, the 45-year-old president of Intermac, a company that made bar-code scanners. Before that, Koogle had spent nine years at the high-tech company Motorola in operations and corporate venture capital, and had, coincidentally, an M.S. and Ph.D. in engineering from Stanford. Like Yang and Filo, Koogle was less interested in how much money he could make than in best serving the company. They also appreciated that Koogle was "willing to put up with a lot of change," as Yang said.

After meeting the Chief Yahoos, Koogle was sufficiently impressed to agree to take the job in August 1995. As he recalled in a Stanford publication, "What struck me immediately was that they had filled a fundamental need and they had done it intuitively. That's what you look for in a business."

Koogle quickly set about to give Yahoo! a strong direction. With the new CEO's help, the company finished putting together its business plan and Yahoo!'s 25 or so employees set

Tim Koogle *(right)* became Yahoo!'s first chief executive officer in August 1995. Koogle had years of business experience, yet he was also able to fit into the loose atmosphere of Yahoo!. Here, he is shown meeting with Hasso Plattner, CEO of the German software company SAP.

about implementing the plan. As was the case at many Internet start-up companies of the day, early Yahoo! employees often accepted low salaries and shares of the company's stock.

The mid-1990s was a time of wild financial enthusiasm, backed by a stock market that seemed to do nothing but go up based largely on the unprecedented growth of Silicon Valley start-ups like Yahoo!. There was money to be made, billions of dollars in some cases, if the examples of Microsoft's Bill Gates and Steve Ballmer and Apple's Steve Jobs and Steve Wozniak were any indication. Computer scientists, engineers, and programmers were more than happy to work impossibly long hours for little money. As holders of company stock, they had a personal investment in Yahoo!'s success. All around them, people were getting rich, and if the price of success was hard work, these were the right people for the job.

It was not uncommon for workers to arrive in the morning to find colleagues asleep under their desks after working through the night. Others seemed to live at the office, its walls painted a garish yellow and purple because that was the cheapest paint available. They worked until they dropped, catching quick naps under their desks before getting back to work. Filo was one of those people, seldom going home, even though he lived only two blocks away. To some, home was a place they saw only when they needed a change of clothes or to take a quick shower.

LAUNCH

The culmination of all these efforts and more was to debut in August 1995.

Still fearful that advertising would drive away users, Yahoo! placed a survey on its home page asking people if they objected to advertisements, new features and promotions, and registering their personal information on the Web site. Expecting 10,000 responses at the most, the poll received 90,000, with more than half of the respondents saying they had no objections to ads or to registering.

In preparation for the new and improved Yahoo!, the number of top categories was reduced to 14 from 19. New features, such as the Reuters news headlines, were added, as was the advertising and a section that allowed Web sites to pay for the

NAVIGATING THE NET

On the *Motley Fool Radio Show*, Jerry Yang said, "Mosaic . . . revolutionized the way people thought about multimedia and the Internet." Mosaic, which first appeared in 1993, was software with a graphical user interface (GUI) that allowed users to search the Internet through either graphics or text. It was created by Marc Andreessen and his team of researchers at the National Center for Supercomputing Applications (NCSA) at the University of Illinois.

In 1994, Andreessen joined with Jim Clark to form the Mosaic Communications Corporation, releasing their first product, Mosaic Netscape 0.9, on October 13, 1994. The number 13 proved lucky for the new company, whose product, soon renamed Netscape Navigator to avoid trademark problems with the NCSA, became the most popular browser on the Web. The company, too, became known as Netscape Communications Corporation.

Andreessen was born on July 8, 1971, in Cedar Falls, Iowa, and was raised in New Lisbon, Wisconsin. He received his bachelor of science degree in computer science from the University of Illinois at Urbana-Champaign, where he also worked at the NCSA. There, he learned of Tim Berners-Lee's 1991 creation of the open architecture protocols for the World Wide Web at the European Laboratory for Particle Physics in Switzerland. Andreessen began to develop, with NCSA employee Eric Bina, a user-friendly browser privilege of being spotlighted. Users who signed up at Yahoo! received a weekly e-mail about hot Web sites.

Unfortunately, with the launch for the new commercial site scheduled for a Monday, Yang had to be the bearer of bad news the Friday before, based on information from Filo. According to Filo, Yahoo!'s technical wizard, there was some question whether the site would work when launched in less than 72 hours. The system, loaded with many new features

that would be compatible with all types of computers, including personal computers and Apples.

In 1993, after graduation and his move west to work in California, Andreessen met Clark, one of the founders of Silicon Graphics, a high-tech company specializing in computer and 3-D graphics. Clark was the one who saw Mosaic's potential as a commercial endeavor and formed the new company with Andreessen as vice president of technology.

Netscape, though distributed free over the Internet, was a smash success and, in 1995, the company had a record-breaking initial public offering that valued it at $2.2 billion, or $71 a share, instantly making Andreessen rich and famous. The Internet was expanding, becoming a great big economic bubble that was making everyone who touched it rich and appeared in no danger of ever stopping. It did not seem to matter that many of these companies were selling nothing but their names.

Netscape would soon lose users to Microsoft's competing browser, Internet Explorer. While many preferred the more stable, user-friendly Netscape, Internet Explorer came bundled with Microsoft's Windows 95 software package and had the software mega-giant's considerable financial and marketplace clout behind it. After losing ground to Internet Explorer for several years, Netscape was acquired by AOL in 1999 for $4.2 billion.

and the ad-hosting software, had never been tested with the number of customers who were expected to flood onto it as soon as it opened its virtual doors.

It was suggested that Filo run a beta test (essentially a test drive by selected customers before the software was released to the general public) of the new system over the weekend. Yahoo! had thousands of users' e-mail addresses on file, and it sent out a mass mailing asking these regular users to preview the new Yahoo!. The test was a success, and Yahoo! launched on schedule.

The new Yahoo! was an immediate success. After a few days, e-mails accusing Yang and Filo of selling out to big business by running ads trickled to a stop, and users accepted the presence of advertising on their favorite Web site. And advertisers were happy to reach alert, intelligent viewers at a bargain price. The first six months after advertising was introduced, Yahoo! attracted more than 70 new advertisers.

Every day, more and more users were introduced to Yahoo! and all of its services. Many Internet companies were being formed with an eye toward being bought out by a larger company or striking it rich with a large IPO. Yahoo! had been born out of an idea and, ignoring the lure of the quick, easy money that a fast buyout would bring them, Yang and Filo had seen their idea through to fruition. Now, they wanted to continue to improve and upgrade what they had built, knowing that their users, like themselves, demanded the level of quality and service to which they had grown accustomed.

Besides the splash Yahoo! was making on the Internet, Yang and Filo were rapidly becoming unlikely stars in their own right, thanks in part to the efforts of the Niehaus Ryan Group public-relations firm. Stories about the Chief Yahoos were appearing everywhere, not only in business and computer trade publications, but also in mainstream magazines like *People* and *Rolling Stone*. More than 600 articles appeared

After the successful commercial launch of Yahoo! in August 1995, Jerry Yang and David Filo began to become unlikely celebrities. In a six-month period, more than 600 articles about them appeared—in industry publications but also in mainstream magazines like *People* and *Rolling Stone*.

in just six months, attracting the attention of companies seeking partnerships with the fledging Internet company.

Through it all, Yang and Filo were sticking to their idealism and keeping the Web as democratic and open for as many people as possible. They recognized that such search engines as AltaVista, Lycos, and others were competitors, but that did not prevent them from linking to these browsers on the Yahoo! homepage. Yang told *BusinessWeek Online* that it was not Yahoo!'s role to restrict its users in any way, saying, "We will let the users decide what's best for them. As we always say, Yahoo! also stands for 'you always have other options!'"

Yang was determined that his users would have no need to ever choose those options. The presence of Reuters news articles was increased, providing links to local and national news, weather, stock quotes, sports scores, and other useful information. Reuters also invested $1 million in Yahoo! for a 2.5 percent share of the company (which it later sold for $80 million). Yahoo! was increasingly becoming a destination for its own content, not just as a search engine. People were making the site their homepage, customized to their individual interests and locations.

And, most important to Yang and Filo, it remained free.

Advertising brought in more and more revenue with each passing quarter. Cosponsorship deals with other companies, like the Visa credit card company, also earned income for Yahoo!. Then, shortly after Yahoo!'s August launch came Netscape's shocking IPO, a moment when everyone involved in Yahoo! must have realized just how large a goldmine they were sitting on.

6

Into the Stratosphere

True to Bob Metcalfe's prediction, Yahoo! had quickly become "the first great Internet brand." Other companies, such as AOL, may have had as high a public profile as Yahoo!, but few had the reputation for integrity and the concern for users that Jerry Yang and David Filo's creation carried. Also, AOL charged a subscription fee for its primary function as a Web portal, and its days as a maverick start-up company were far behind it. America Online was even then on track to become large enough to buy media giant Time Warner in a deal worth $164 billion in 2000.

Yahoo!, on the other hand, stayed true to its democratic roots, and its employees stayed away from extravagant spending at a time when most Internet start-ups saw millions of dollars run through their fingers without producing much in the way of products or services. For 1995, Yahoo! reported a loss of $634,000 on revenues, or earnings, of $1.4 million. That loss was modest compared with the operation of many Internet companies that spent their money on offices, fancy décor, and

67

salaries for their executives. Offices, as evidenced from conditions at 110 Pioneer Way, were not a priority, nor were items like cars and fancy clothes.

Yang and Filo each earned a salary of $40,000 in 1995. Many executives took as much as half their pay in company stock, which turned out to be compensation worth far more than any salary they could have received at the time. Filo continued to drive his rusted-out Toyota, admitting to a reporter for *Metroactive*, "I do need to get the thing fixed, but there is just no time." The office roof continued to leak, the cheap yellow and purple paint still adorned the walls, and with T-shirts and shorts the standard office dress, no one was spending a fortune on clothing. Money was spent only on what was necessary, which were usually items to help the company grow and become profitable. No one expected a start-up company the size of Yahoo! to turn a profit for several years.

A BUMP IN THE NETSCAPE

Word of the Netscape initial public offering (IPO) was followed, not long after, by the browser dropping Yahoo! as its official search engine—Yahoo! lost its prominent placement on Netscape's directory page. Another search engine had offered Netscape too good a deal to replace Yahoo!.

Yahoo!'s investors viewed this change with alarm. Without the support of that direct link from powerhouse Netscape, the search engine's once bright future suddenly seemed in jeopardy. Advertisers paid for the space they bought on Yahoo! based on the number of viewers the site attracted. The more people who clicked onto Yahoo!, the more money Yahoo! could charge its advertisers.

With the looming threat of Steve Case's AOL developing its own search engine and the host of other competitors popping up across the Internet, Yahoo! looked as though it was in

In the early years at Yahoo!, the atmosphere was casual, from its founders on down. The employees at Yahoo! avoided extravagant spending—on themselves and their surroundings—during the Internet boom of the 1990s, even when many similar companies were burning through money.

trouble. There was concern in the financial and business community that this seemingly charmed start-up might be turning into just another casualty on the fast track of the mid-1990s Internet boom.

Yang and Filo kept calm and, more important, maintained a steady, friendly relationship with Netscape. At the time, Yang told reporters, "I'm pretty optimistic that we'll work with Netscape again," knowing that the other company would soon realize that it was not good business to restrict itself to a single search engine even if it was being paid a very high fee.

Being Asian American: EDUCATION AND DRIVE

In 2005, the Asia Society honored five prominent Asian-American entrepreneurs who were born overseas and came to the United States in their youth. In his introduction of honoree Jerry Yang, presenter David Ho, director and chief executive officer of the Aaron Diamond AIDS Research Center, said, "Here I am a scientist, about to present the award to an engineer. Our prototypic Chinese parents must be proud."

Dr. Ho's joke elicited laughter from the largely Asian-American audience, who understood the importance that their parents, whether first-, second-, or later-generation Asian Americans, placed on learning and achievement. And it seems to be that Chinese tradition of study combined with the American drive for success that connects the Taiwanese-born Yang to his dual heritage.

When Jerry was two years old, his father died. His widowed mother, Lily, found it difficult to find work in her chosen profession, and she taught Yang to always be practical in his life and his choices. At a Silicon Valley conference of computer and Internet professionals, Yang shared his mother's old-world advice: "If you are served food on the table, better eat it; you may not know when your next meal will be again!"

Lily Yang's values have stayed with Jerry his entire life. In an interview with AsianConnections.com, he said, "The key thing my mother emphasized is the education—we didn't grow up wealthy and therefore studying and getting the best education possible was the primary goal. Education is something that you keep for the rest of your life, and no one can take that away from you."

Besides, establishing a precedent in which high fees for links to browsers, Internet portals, and other search engines became the norm was dangerous. Companies like Yahoo! would be

> Every immigrant comes to the United States with a dream of the promise this country offers. Ten-year-old Yang Chih-Yuan surely had his dreams when he arrived here. The reality is he became the co-founder of one of the largest Internet companies in the world and a billionaire before the age of 40. AsianConnections.com asked Yang about the issue of the corporate glass ceiling, or the lack of opportunity for Asians above a certain level, based on the relatively low number of Asian Americans running American companies. The interviewer wondered if he had deliberately chosen a "less traditional path" to land at the top of the corporate ladder.
>
> Yang replied, "You can never 'plan' to take the path I did. . . . My goal was to get the best education I can and prepare for any opportunities that make sense. If I didn't become a founder of a company, I would have joined a start-up and tried to make a difference there. I'm not so concerned with title and position, but I am concerned with making a difference. I believe as long as people can make an impact, then the glass ceiling will eventually break because the marketplace of ideas will force the smartest, brightest, and (most) impactful people to rise to the top."
>
> Goldsea.com, a Web site devoted to the Asian-American experience, called Yang "a fun-loving geek with two degrees from Stanford and a billion-plus net worth. Best of all, he's the crazily grinning face of the Internet's most popular brand. That makes Jerry Yang a power geek . . . and as the hippest of ubergeeks, Jerry Yang has done more than anyone to take Asians out of nerdsville and turn them into icons of savvy tech fortunes."

unable to turn a profit and stay in business if the cost of accessibility to users was too high.

The entire Internet industry was no doubt watching to see how being dropped by Netscape would affect Yahoo!. In the first week, the site saw a slight dip in traffic. The following week, the numbers bounced back and then climbed even higher than before. Far from suffering, traffic to Yahoo!. had gone up. By now, regular Yahoo! users had the site bookmarked and did not need to go through Netscape to find it, while word of mouth and online bulletin boards continued to spread the news about Yahoo!.

The following year, Netscape again changed its policy for including search engines on its page. It would link to several search engines, each of which paid the same, more reasonable fee. Being back on Netscape only accelerated Yahoo!'s growth, which in turn made Yahoo! again look attractive to new investors. At the rate the company was going, Yahoo! would soon be looking at an IPO of its own.

"PRIMARILY, WE'RE A BRAND"

With Tim Koogle in place as CEO, Philip Monego left Yahoo! in September 1995 to look after other interests. By that time, the company had 25 employees, 20,000 Web pages receiving millions of hits every day, dozens of advertisers, and a growing reputation among users and business leaders as a strong, well-managed company. Monego had begun to negotiate with Japanese and American software and publishing companies he felt fit Yang's strategy going forward, companies that could provide content and financial clout for Yahoo!.

Growth demanded money, and money, at this stage of Yahoo!'s development, was unlikely to come from profits. That money needed to come from outside investors. To convince these investors that Yahoo! was a good buy, Yang knew he had to remained focused on what was important. "Primarily, we're a brand," Yang said in *Inside Yahoo!*. "We're trying to promote the brand and build the product so that it has reliability, pizzazz, and credibility. The focus of all the business deals we are doing right now is not on revenues but on our brand."

The strategy worked. In November, Reuters bought its $1 million, 2.5 percent share, while magazine publisher Ziff Davis and Japanese software distributor Softbank put up $2 million for a 5 percent share each. These deals gave Yahoo! partners in the Japanese and European markets, furthering its reach and extending its brand. Ziff Davis discovered the added value of the Yahoo! name when it changed the title of its one-year-old magazine *ZD Internet Life* to *Yahoo! Internet Life* and saw circulation quickly double to 200,000 copies an issue.

Wall Street, the center of the U.S. financial marketplace, had taken notice of Yahoo! and the rest of the Internet. The large investment-banking houses, which helped companies put together their IPOs and sell shares of stock to the public, were themselves earning small fortunes for their services. One investment-banking firm in particular, Goldman Sachs, had its eye on Yahoo!. The bank had already handled IPOs for several Internet service providers and was now looking at companies that offered service and content as the next step in the growth of the Web.

Michael Parekh was in charge of analyzing the strengths and weaknesses of Yahoo! for Goldman Sachs. As he said in *Inside Yahoo!*, "We were looking at the Yahoo! people, and they were the only ones thinking about online services built on top of search and directory, and from day one, they were fixated on the consumer—whereas the founders of almost every company were thinking about this from a technology standpoint. Yahoo!'s people said, 'We'll just license whatever is the best technology and build services around it to take advantage of the traffic.' That's the model that resonated with me, because I'd seen it work for AOL and CompuServe."

FAST TRACK TO IPO

Yahoo! was not the only search engine about to go public. Two competitors, Excite and Lycos, were also planning IPOs. Yang and Filo knew that they had to get themselves on the market. There were serious economic reasons for doing so, but to Yang, the main reason had to do with perception: Yahoo! was the online search-engine leader, a role he refused to relinquish.

Jerry Yang is shown visiting the NASDAQ stock exchange in New York City in March 2005. On April 12, 1996, Yahoo! had its initial public offering on the NASDAQ exchange. On that day, Yahoo! became a company valued at $850 million, and Yang himself was worth $130 million.

As he explained in the book *The Internet Bubble*, Yang feared that, if the other companies went public well before Yahoo!, his company would lose its advantage. "Not only would they have the extra cash, but they could also use the stock as currency to acquire other companies. To have Excite and Lycos out there consolidating the market while we couldn't would've been a huge mistake." Besides, Yang believed that Yahoo! was not only the superior product but that investors were looking for companies run by true believers like himself and Filo, rather than greedy businessmen in it for a quick profit.

As Yahoo! was contemplating its IPO, the company moved to a larger, although not significantly better, office space in February 1996 at 635 Vaqueros in Sunnyvale, California. The Web site was receiving more than 6 million page views a day, double the traffic it had less than six months earlier.

On April 12, 1996, Yahoo! went public—10 days after Lycos and eight days after Excite. Its stock (listed as YHOO on the NASDAQ, or the National Association of Securities Dealers Automated Quotations, an American stock exchange) originally sold for $13 a share, with the price reaching as high as $43 before ending the first day of trading at $33. In a single day, Yahoo! had become a company valued at roughly $850 million. Lycos and Excite could only claim $241 million and $206 million, respectively. Infoseek, another search engine that had its IPO the following June, came in at $259 million. All were considered successes. Only Yahoo! took off beyond all expectations. Shareholders, including those early employees and executives who took company stock instead of salaries, became rich in the blink of an eye.

Yang and Filo, who had gone from living on $19,000 a year as graduate students to $40,000 a year as Chief Yahoos of their own company, were multimillionaires, all in less than two years. They were suddenly worth $130 million each, a staggering fortune that would, amazingly, be eclipsed over the next four years, until Yahoo! stock reached its peak of $237.50 a share in January 2000.

"Being a core part of a business that affects many people is different and takes some getting used to, but I am surprised at how little has changed in my life. Dave and I are still the same old guys who dress badly and drive beat-up cars," Yang wrote in *Yahoo! Unplugged*. The truth of that statement could be seen in the fact that, despite his newfound wealth, Filo did not even bother to move from the apartment in Mountain View that he shared with a roommate.

That Yahoo! was changing how things were done made the Wall Street establishment nervous enough. The company needed to project the image of mature, stable hands leading the way to inspire confidence in investors, advertisers, and commercial partners alike. Yahoo!'s new brand manager hoped to have people see Yahoo! as a media company, "a place that would connect anybody with anything they needed or anybody they needed."

With all the funding it could need for expansion and the exploration of new territories, both geographical and technological, Yahoo! was launched in Japan and Canada. These sites featured content and listings tailored to those nations, just as regional pages like Yahoo! New York directed users to a city's attractions and services.

Advertising continued to account for most of Yahoo!'s revenue, but it was by no means the only source. Efforts to make money from the site were constantly being tried, such as selling links to stores and receiving an additional payment for every Yahoo! surfer clicking through to that store. Businesses paid to be on Yahoo! so that it could remain free for its users.

And Yahoo!'s users appreciated it; by the first half of 1998, Yahoo! was hosting more than 30 million visitors a month,

After Yahoo! went public, it began to expand into international markets. Yahoo! Japan was launched in 1996 and went on to become the country's most-visited Web portal. Here, a sign promoting Yahoo! Japan looms over a Tokyo street.

WEB CRAWLING

A search engine is composed of three main parts, beginning with the "spider," which is a specialized software robot designed to follow Internet links to pages that have not yet been indexed (that is, a list made of their contents) and pages in need of updating. Spiders search millions of Web pages on an ongoing basis, compiling lists of the words and images appearing on the Internet in a process known as web crawling.

The results of the spider's Web crawling are then added to the second part of the search engine, the index. This is the master list, or catalog, of everything the spiders have been able to discover on their cyber-journeys.

Spiders are able to penetrate the World Wide Web so thoroughly because, as they search a Web site, they follow all the links they find there.

To access the results of a search query, the search engine calls upon the search interface, the final component in this complex machine, which creates the list that the user may choose from. But far from posting a mere list of results, most search engines perform a variety of functions to instantly verify and organize the information to make it most useful. It checks the spelling of a query, then looks to see if the query matches anything listed in related databases.

Next, a list of relevant pages, ranked by content, frequency of usage, and other factors, are gathered, as are any advertisements connected to the query. Finally, all these links and suggestions for relevant information, goods, and services are displayed for the user to click on and follow, wherever on the World Wide Web they may lead.

At Yahoo!, unlike other search engines, the listings are compiled by live people who are hired to surf the Internet and bookmark what they find. This adds a very human touch to the listings, with which other search engines, relying entirely on robotic spiders to gather their information, cannot compete.

downloading an astonishing 100 million pages a day. Advertisers, who paid Yahoo! $67 million in 1997, were likewise thrilled with the audience the Web site delivered.

Yahoo! moved to larger, nicer offices about a mile (6 km) down the road from its old Sunnyvale headquarters, eventually filling 100,000 square feet (9,290 square meters) of office space. And Yang at last spent some of his newfound wealth on himself, buying a $2 million house overlooking San Francisco Bay and a car. At the rate things were going, he could be reasonably sure that Yahoo! was here to stay.

Twenty-First Century Yahoos

Yahoo! was now recognized as one of the strongest brands on the World Wide Web and, more important, it still cared about its users. "We will absolutely have to stay ahead of what our users want and be able to continue to bring them services and products that make sense," Jerry Yang told listeners of the *Motley Fool Radio Show* in 1999.

As Goldman Sachs analyst Michael Parekh had noted when looking over the company before its initial public offering, Yahoo! did not mind licensing the best available technology to build services around as long as it served users and helped increase traffic to the site. Now, flush with cash, Yahoo! did not have to license technology; the company could simply buy it outright, acquiring Web sites that provided services Yahoo! wished to carry—or that did a better job than what Yahoo! was already doing.

Yahoo! bought almost 20 rival Internet companies, including the job-search site Hotjobs.com; the online media company Broadcast.com; and the Internet community GeoCities.

Besides giving Yahoo! these sites and services, the acquisitions also gave the company a base of devoted users who would now be spending time on Yahoo!. Plus, it did not hurt to be taking competing Web sites off the Internet.

Yahoo! continued to look to the future, even if Yang and David Filo sometimes found themselves rooted firmly in the present, as was the case with their computer equipment. The Chief Yahoos stuck with their old personal computers, claiming that they were comfortable with the machines and that it was too much of a bother to upgrade. In truth, they wanted to use the same equipment as most of Yahoo!'s customers. This way, they were able to experience Yahoo! the same way as any surfer on their old, slow dial-up modems.

THE BUBBLE BURSTS

Throughout the 1990s, the Internet experienced wild, runaway expansion that saw the creation of thousands of Web sites and untold trillions of dollars in economic growth. The Internet was an expanding bubble that seemed unstoppable, and everyone with a catchy name for a Web site was jumping on and hoping to grab some of that vast wealth for themselves.

The problem was, most of that wealth existed only on paper, in the stock-market valuations of all of these start-up Internet companies. In their enthusiasm for the marketplace offered by the new technology, people forgot the most basic of business principles: To be successful, a business needs to sell a product that people need or want. Too many start-ups had nothing to sell but an image on which the creators hoped to sell advertising until even larger companies bought them out for ridiculously large sums of money. Stock prices for almost every Internet company, including Yahoo!, were greatly overinflated.

Added to the overblown sense of well-being in the computer and Internet world was the coming of the year 2000. There was widespread fear that at 12:01 A.M. on January 1, 2000, computers around the world, unable to process the date "2000" would crash. This so-called Y2K bug (for "Year 2000") created a deluge of spending in the late 1990s by governments and businesses to fix the problem by creating new software and often by replacing their outdated computers entirely.

As the Y2K turmoil settled down, the technology business slowed. Those buying new equipment had done so in advance of Y2K and a whole industry of consultants, programmers, and software engineers specializing in the problem found they had fixed themselves out of work.

A look at the stock-market ticker in March 2000 would not have revealed a problem; the NASDAQ, the stock exchange on which Yahoo! traded, was at an all-time high of 5,132.52. Yahoo!'s stock was trading at $233 a share. It had hit its high in January, at $237.50 a share.

This bubble, though, reached its limit and when it burst in 2000, it shook most of those who had grabbed hold in search of a quick buck. Companies closed their doors by the hundreds, and Web sites disappeared. Brands that had become overnight sensations for their advertisements or slogans sank into oblivion under their own overinflated values.

The plunge lasted until October 2002, sending the NASDAQ plummeting back down to 1,108.49, about one-fifth its value at the height of the bubble. Investors were left with stocks, once worth hundreds of dollars, now worth pennies—if they could have found anyone to buy them. Yahoo!'s stock hit a low of $8 a share.

An estimated $8 trillion was lost in the crash of 2000, but Yahoo!, despite the difficult times, managed to hold on. During this time, Yang continued to push the promise of the Internet. In one speech in April 2000 before the National Press Club in

Traders in the NASDAQ 100 Futures trading pit in Chicago tossed paper into the air after a wild day on April 14, 2000. The index dropped 361.58 points that day, then a one-day record. The Internet industry—Yahoo! included—was in the midst of a severe downturn.

Washington, he said, "At the end of last year, a hundred million people in the United States were on the Net. In 2003, the number will double in the United States to 200 million. Audience size and growth is what this is all about. You're seeing the transformation of changing people's lives and behavior. I always look at those numbers. If they're still going up, we have a tremendous opportunity."

Through smart planning and difficult economic decisions, including laying off hundreds of employees for a savings of more than $30 million a year, Yahoo! was able to weather the crash of 2000. In addition, through the aggressive pursuit of

(continues on page 86)

Other Notable Individuals

ANDREW CHI-CHIH YAO

Computer scientists operate under Moore's Law, which says that computer-processor speeds double every 18 months. This observation was first made in 1965 by Intel co-founder Gordon E. Moore, based on the trend that the silicon-chip manufacturer first noticed in 1958 and that continues, more than 40 years later, to hold true.

However, according to a 1999 U.S. Department of Defense study, "This growth will reach a limit by the year 2020," at which point processing speeds will have reached the limitations of the laws of physics. "Quantum computation is one proposed alternative to this limitation," the paper continued. "Recent experiments have provided a proof of concept for quantum computation, and some researchers believe that a working model could be developed within a reasonable time period. This success has caused a marked increase in the interest in quantum computers and their proposed potential."

For all the advancements in speed and miniaturization, the basis for the computer's operation has changed little since it was introduced in the 1940s: an electronic signal moving along a physical medium. But according to Professor Andrew Chi-Chih Yao of the Chinese University of Hong Kong, the era of the silicon chip is coming to an end. What will replace it is not known for certain yet, but whatever it is, it will flow from Yao's specialty, theoretical computing.

Theoretical computing, according to a press release from the Chinese University of Hong Kong, "is a discipline that tries to bring fundamental breakthrough to computing by studying the very foundations of computation. In time, it may bring us new computers that will completely redefine our notion of computing."

"If successfully developed, quantum computers would set off another scientific revolution," Yao said in the same press release. "They can solve problems that currently require billions of years of computing time. Most of the encryption methods now rely heavily on their complexity of computation; therefore whether they be banking transactions or military secrets, [they] will be cracked by quantum computers easily."

Yao was born in Shanghai, China, in 1946 and received a bachelor of science in physics from National Taiwan University in 1967, a Ph.D. in physics from Harvard University in 1972, and a Ph.D. in computer science from the University of Illinois in 1975. He served on the faculties of the Massachusetts Institute of Technology, Stanford University, and the University of California, Berkeley, before joining Princeton University in 1986. Yao, whose research has included work on analysis of algorithms, computational complexity, cryptography, and quantum computing, received the A.M. Turing Award in 2000 for contributions to the theory of computation. In 2004, he became a professor at Tsinghua University in Beijing and a Distinguished Professor-at-Large at the Chinese University of Hong Kong.

While Yao continues his research into the next generation of computers, he is also helping create the next generation of computer scientists. According to *The New York Times* of October 28, 2005, "China wants to transform its top universities into the world's best within a decade, and it is spending billions of dollars to woo big-name scholars like Dr. Yao and build first-class research laboratories." China's efforts were yielding results: In 1978, only 1.4 percent of the college-age population was enrolled in higher education. That figure had risen to almost 20 percent by 2005.

While Yao's research remains at the forefront of the computer sciences, he decided that, as a teacher, he was needed at a more remedial level. Finding that Chinese undergraduates were not receiving the training they needed to be successful graduate students, he decided to teach at that level. "You can't just say I'll only do the cutting-edge stuff," he said. "You've got to teach the basics really well first."

(continued from page 83)

new advertisers and other business opportunities, Yahoo! grew even larger than ever.

In 2005, during a dinner presented by the Asia Society, Yang spoke about the Internet bubble with emcee Lisa Ling, showing his strong belief in Yahoo!:

> It was definitely one of the toughest times I think for our industry. In a way the most healthy as well, because the companies that have emerged from the bubble are probably the strongest companies and even probably stronger than they were going in. As for Yahoo!, we never felt that the basic fundamentals of what made Yahoo! great and obviously what made the Internet great was going away. . . . You look at our brand, even during the toughest times, people really felt that Yahoo! made their lives a little better on the Internet.

TERRY SEMEL AND YAHOO!

As Yahoo!'s stock slumped, the company's board realized that a change at the top was needed. On February 27, 2001, chief executive officer Tim Koogle resigned. Two months later, Terry Semel, the former head of Warner Bros., took over as Yahoo!'s CEO. Semel, with his background in the traditional old media of Hollywood, seemed a strange choice to run an Internet company, but what he did not know about technology he more than made up for with his understanding of business. Yang had pushed for Semel to be CEO. They had met two years earlier and had since forged a friendship, meeting for lunch every couple of months.

Semel's task as CEO was twofold. He had to persuade advertisers that Yahoo! could deliver a solid return for them. He also had to reduce the company's dependence on ad dollars by coming up with new sources of revenue.

He began to help Yahoo! find its direction by combining 44 business departments into four and focusing on the development of a new search engine. He also had Yahoo! buy Overture, an Internet company that was the first to successfully provide a

As Yahoo!'s stock continued to drop in 2001, Terry Semel (*above*) replaced Tim Koogle as CEO. With his years of experience as head of a Hollywood studio, Semel seemed an unusual choice to run an Internet company.

pay-for-placement search service. Overture offered advertisers the option of bidding on how much they would pay to appear at the top of the results in response to a specific search. The advertiser paid the bid amount every time a searcher clicked on a link to the advertiser's Web site. Under Semel's watch, Yahoo also bought the search engines AltaVista, AllTheWeb, and Inktomi in 2003.

Semel's first three years in charge were successful enough that the price of Yahoo!'s stock nearly tripled. But even with all of Semel's efforts to force the company to take and maintain a direction, Yahoo! remained adrift in 2005, still trying to be too many things to too many people. And a new giant had emerged in the search-engine field—Google.

Yahoo! may have been a household name and was the routine choice of hundreds of millions of users. In fact, Yahoo! is more popular than Google—with 500 million monthly visitors to Google's 380 million visitors, according to a February 2007 article in *Time* magazine. But when many of those people wanted to do an online search, they clicked over to Google to do it, and that made Google more profitable than Yahoo!. According to a *BusinessWeek* article, Google had 49 percent of all search-oriented ad business in 2005, up from 33 percent the year before.

As in any other mass media, such as television, radio, and newspapers, advertisers pay to promote their goods or services on Web sites. The price they pay to appear on a site depends on the number of people who regularly visit the site. The more people who visit a site, the higher the rates that site can charge to advertisers. Online advertising, though, is not only about the number of people who visit a site; it is also about how these visitors *behave* once they arrive. Are they regular visitors? How many pages do they view? How long do they spend on each page? Do they click on advertising banners that link to the advertisers' sites? On all these vital questions, the answers kept coming up in favor of rival Google.

YAHOO! IN CHINA

Despite the competition from Google, Yahoo! remained a considerable force. Part of Yahoo!'s success came from its foray into international markets. Ten days after Yahoo! had gone public in 1996, it launched Yahoo! Japan—the first effort by an American Internet guide to establish a foreign site. Yahoo! Japan would become one of the company's more profitable enterprises. Nearby in Asia, China was seen as the market of the future for many businesses, although one that raised plenty of concerns.

The 1.3 billion citizens of China offer a difficult but irresistible target for twenty-first-century multinational corporations. On the one hand, the People's Republic of China represents a vast market for products as diverse as Coca-Cola and McDonald's, Levi jeans, and state-of-the-art electronics. On the other hand, the country's restrictive laws and routine censorship made it difficult to do business the way most companies were accustomed.

The situation was much more difficult for an Internet portal and search engine like Yahoo! than it was for a fast-food franchise like KFC. China has an authoritative government. The Internet, however, had developed democratically and according to the natural laws of capitalism. Yahoo!, in particular, was created to be an open democracy. Yang always said, "We will let the users decide what's best for them." His motto remained, "Yahoo! also stands for 'you always have other options.'"

In China, though, options were few even if the once staunchly Communist nation had begun to adopt limited, but significant, economic reforms in the 1990s in an attempt to be competitive in the changing world economy. This opened the door to many companies and, on May 4, 1998, Yahoo! launched

Yahoo! Chinese, its thirteenth non-English site. (The name of the site later became Yahoo! China.)

To do so, Yahoo! had to first get around Chinese law that then prohibited foreign investment in Internet content providers. Yang struck up a partnership deal with a Chinese company that would provide all the content while Yahoo! supplied all the technology and the hardware and software to run the system.

In a deal announced in August 2005, Yahoo! shored up its commitment to the Chinese market by combining with China's leading e-commerce company, Alibaba.com. Under the agreement, Yahoo! China became a part of the Chinese company, with Yahoo! investing an additional $1 billion for a 40 percent share of Alibaba.com. The merger created one of the largest Internet companies in China.

Not all of the news out of China was good for Yahoo!. Reporters Without Borders, an international organization dedicated to the right of freedom of opinion, thought, and expression, had condemned Yahoo! when it had joined other Internet companies in agreeing to restrictions on subjects forbidden by the Chinese government. Other problems arose in 2005 when it was revealed that Yahoo! gave e-mail information about Chinese journalist Shi Tao to China's security forces. The Chinese government used that information to charge the reporter with revealing state secrets and sentenced him to 10 years in prison.

Yahoo! responded to attacks over Shi Tao's arrest by saying that the company had no way of knowing what the Chinese government was investigating when it asked for the information. It could have been trying to stop a spammer or someone trying to spread a computer virus, or it might have been in pursuit of terrorists.

Yang said that the company had to obey the local laws. "We did not know what they wanted information for," he told reporters in 2005. "We are not told what they look for. If they give us the proper documentation in a court order, we give them things that satisfy local laws."

It was later revealed that Yahoo! officials in China had received a subpoena-like document that referred to suspected "illegal provisions of state secrets." In November 2007, Yang and the company's general counsel, Michael J. Callahan, faced scathing criticism when they were called before the House Foreign Affairs Committee in Congress. The committee's chairman, Representative Tom Lantos of California, said, "While technologically and financially you are giants, morally you are pygmies." He told the two men to apologize to Shi Tao's mother, who was sitting behind them at the hearing.

That same month, Yahoo! established a human-rights fund to provide humanitarian and legal aid to dissidents imprisoned for expressing their views online. A few months later, Yang asked U.S. Secretary of State Condoleezza Rice to help get Shi Tao and another jailed journalist, Wang Xiaoning, out of prison. In his letter to Rice, as cited in an Associated Press article, Yang wrote that Yahoo! "deeply regrets the circumstances" that led to the jailing of the two journalists, adding that it ran against company values. "We know we have an important role to play in advocating for the release of these political dissidents," the letter continued. "We are also aware of the limits of private American companies engaging in foreign policy." As of July 2009, Shi Tao remained in prison.

In 2007, Yahoo! China was involved in another controversy, this time involving a battle in the Chinese courts over music piracy. The lawsuit, brought by the International Federation of Phonographic Industries, accused Yahoo! China of violating copyrights by allowing links between its search engine and Web sites that illegally copy songs.

A lower court ruled in April 2007 that Yahoo! China facilitated infringement of copyrights. Yahoo! China appealed

Jerry Yang turned around to address Gao Qin Sheng, the mother of jailed Chinese journalist Shi Tao, during a hearing before the House Foreign Affairs Committee in November 2007. Yahoo! China had given e-mail information to the Chinese authorities, leading to Shi Tao's arrest.

the decision, claiming it was not responsible for the content on other Web sites, but the higher court rejected that argument.

While the Chinese economy becomes more and more central to the world economy, it is expected that China will one day find its way to a more democratic way of governing. Until then, the traditions of the old ways will continue to bump heads with the new generation of global e-connectivity and e-commerce.

FROM CHIEF YAHOO TO CHIEF EXECUTIVE OFFICER

More than a decade after its founding, the problem most people saw with Yahoo! was that it had grown too large, even after CEO Terry Semel had consolidated the business units. Yahoo! was, according to the article "How Yahoo! Aims to Reboot" in the February 2, 2007, issue of *Time* magazine, "a company that has divided its attention among dozens of products and services." The article quoted Drew Neisser, CEO of the Renegade Marketing Group advertising agency, as saying, "Yahoo! is many things to so many people, whereas the beauty of Google is that, at the end of the day, it's search done well."

Under Semel, Yahoo! was trying, in the minds of many, to decide what it wanted to be when it grew up. Was it a search engine? An advertising platform? A content provider? An online community? Some felt these efforts to decide the direction the company should take had caused it to lose even more focus. In a company memo that was leaked to the public, Yahoo! senior vice president Brad Garlinghouse likened the situation to spreading a finite amount of peanut butter on an ever-growing slice of bread. "The result," he wrote, according to the *Time* article, was "a thin layer of investment spread across everything we do and thus we focus on nothing in particular. I hate peanut butter. We all should." He went on to note that "we lack decisiveness (and) we are held hostage by our analysis paralysis." In other words, he wanted the company to make up its mind.

By early 2007, analysts were looking at Yahoo! and beginning to predict that, unless the company found a way to catch up with or overtake Google, both it and Semel were in trouble. The inability to keep up with Google had had a disastrous effect on Yahoo!'s stock price—it had fallen 36 percent in 2006. For all that Semel had accomplished during his six years as CEO, including increasing Yahoo!'s annual revenues by 900 percent and adding $30 billion to the company's net worth, the stock market and Yahoo! investors would only watch the company's stock price slide for so long before they wanted change.

As *Time* reported on June 19, "When you compete against the Godzilla that is Google, even modest slip-ups can cost you a job. A sliding stock doesn't sit well, and second place in the Web world isn't good enough."

That week, Semel announced he was leaving his position as Yahoo!'s CEO. His replacement: co-founder Jerry Yang.

8

Looking to the Future

When it was announced in June 2007 that Jerry Yang was becoming the CEO at Yahoo!, the reaction was positive but reserved. "There's probably no better person than a founder to rescue a troubled company," Ned May, lead analyst for Outsell, a California-based research and consulting firm, said in *Time* magazine, "but there may also be no better person to drive it into the ground. History is going to look favorably on (Apple Computer co-founder and CEO) Steve Jobs, but there are lots of unwritten stories where founders weren't successful." David Smith, technology analyst at Gartner, said that Yang might have too much influence for Yahoo!'s own good. "Founders have a special place in every company and tend to be listened to longer than they should," he said in *Time*.

On the day he became CEO, Yang said in an interview with *The New York Times* that his main tasks would be to reinvigorate the company and attract top talent. "We have a very clear strategy in place, and we are executing it," he said. Yang intended to continue to use the business model developed by

Terry Semel—to sell search and display advertising on the Yahoo! portal; to sell ads on the Web sites of partners; and to become an ad broker on sites across the Web. "I believe that Yahoo! has all the assets it takes to win, and we're well-positioned to do just that," Yang added.

Still, many analysts speculated that Yahoo! might join up with another company. The *Time* article ended with one analyst saying that "Microsoft and Yahoo! have a long history of being partners, and they're likely to get closer. We wouldn't be surprised to see a joint venture emerge."

YAHOO! FOR SALE?

Rather than a joint venture, however, Microsoft came forward with an offer to buy Yahoo! in February 2008 in a deal that would have been worth $44.6 billion. Under the deal, Microsoft would have paid $31 a share for Yahoo!, which was trading around $19 a share at the time. Yang refused the proposal, perhaps remembering how he felt about Microsoft more than a decade earlier, when the powerful software giant was an alarming presence looming over the computer and Internet landscape. "You never, ever want to compete with Microsoft," Yang said in 1997. "And even if they want to compete with you, you run away and do something else."

Yang also thought the offer was too low. "We have a huge market opportunity—and are uniquely positioned to capitalize on it," Yang wrote in a February letter to shareholders, as cited in *The New York Times*. "The global online advertising market is projected to grow from $45 billion in 2007 to $75 billion in 2010. And we are moving quickly to take advantage of what we see as a unique window of time in the growth—and evolution—of this market to build market share and to create value for stockholders."

At an industry meeting later that month, he said that the bid for Yahoo! and the efforts to fend it off had set off an exciting time within the company. "In many ways it has been a galvanizing event for all of Yahoo!," Yang said, according to *The New York Times*. He also spoke about his vision for Yahoo!. "It's hard to believe that it has been only 13 years since Yahoo! started. The journey has been anything but boring. We are on the cusp of something more interesting as we go forward. . . . We talk about having Yahoo! being the starting point, again, for the Internet."

The standoff between Microsoft and Yahoo! continued for weeks. Microsoft later increased its offer to $33 a share, but Yang was reportedly holding out for $37 a share. As *Time* magazine noted on May 3, "Although Jerry Yang repeatedly said that he would consider Microsoft's bid, he showed little interest in actually making a deal, instead focusing his energies on finding alternative suitors. Now, Yang appears to have gotten his way: Less than a month after threatening a hostile takeover if Yahoo! declined its initial $44.6 billion offer, Microsoft CEO Steve Ballmer formally withdrew his company's offer." The article also quoted a statement from Yang, "With the distraction of Microsoft's unsolicited proposal now behind us, we will be able to focus all of our energies on executing the most important transition in our history."

Next, Yang made a deal with rival Google to share advertising revenues across the two sites. The deal could have been worth $250 million to $450 million in the first year to Yahoo!. Under the proposal, Google would deliver ads next to some of Yahoo!'s search results and on some of its Web sites. Government regulators, however, worried that the combined power of these two Internet giants would give them an unfair advantage over small companies competing for the same advertising dollars. The fear was that they could offer advertisers rates that smaller Web sites could not match, eventually driving those rivals out of business. Under pressure from the regulators over those antitrust concerns, Google decided not to go through with the deal.

Many shareholders were frustrated with the collapse of the Microsoft deal, especially as Yahoo!'s stock continued to tumble. In October, Yahoo! announced that its revenues for

Jerry Yang gave a thumbs-up sign as he left a Yahoo! shareholders' meeting in August 2008 in San Jose, California. Yang was under pressure as many shareholders were frustrated that a bid by Microsoft to buy Yahoo! had fallen through.

the third quarter had fallen from the previous quarter. Yang was forced to lay off 10 percent of Yahoo!'s 15,000 workers. Shareholders were questioning whether Yang should be running the company he helped create. Soon enough, Yang apparently agreed.

On November 17, 2008, Yahoo! announced that Yang would be stepping down as CEO—a move that was "mutual" and "in progress for a while," according to *The New York Times.* In a statement, Yang said, "Having set Yahoo! on a new, more open path, the time is right for me to transition the CEO role and our global talent to a new leader."

Yang was not going far, however. As he explained in a memo to his staff, "All of you know that I have always and will always bleed purple," a reference to Yahoo!'s corporate color and his dedication to the company. Yang would remain on Yahoo!'s board of directors and help in the search for the person who would replace him as CEO. More important, he would be returning to his earlier position as Chief Yahoo.

GIVING TO THE COMMUNITY

While much of Yang's life has been consumed by Yahoo! since he and Filo started it in 1994, he has managed to devote plenty of time to the betterment of the community. Yang and his wife, Akiko Yamazaki, who have two daughters, have supported many education and arts organizations in the San Francisco Bay Area, including the Asian Art Museum, the East Asian Library at the University of California, Berkeley, and the San Francisco Ballet. They are also supporters of the Asian Pacific Fund, donating multiyear gifts to its Annual Fund. Yang serves as a board member for the Asian Pacific Fund.

In 2007, Yang and Yamazaki pledged $75 million to enhance multidisciplinary programs at Stanford University, their alma mater. Of their gift, $50 million went to cover construction costs for the university's new Environment and Energy

Building. Another $5 million was earmarked for construction of the high-tech Learning and Knowledge Center for the School of Medicine. The remaining money will go toward projects still to be determined.

Yamazaki said she and her husband welcomed the chance to make a substantial contribution to the Environment and Energy Building, which was completed in December 2007 and serves as the hub of environmental studies at Stanford.

"The future is in interdisciplinary problem-solving," said Yamazaki, who is a director of the Wildlife Conservation Network in Los Altos, California. "This building and the programs

SEARCHING THE FUTURE

We have come to expect much from our computers and the tools we use on them. In particular, we have come to rely on the Internet search engine to answer just about any question that comes to mind, from the name of the actor who appeared in a movie you saw last night on television to research for your science paper.

Search engines have become powerful, accurate, and fast, finding tens or hundreds of thousands of matches, or hits, to a query in the blink of an eye. The word *bluebird* typed into the Yahoo! search box yielded 37,600,000 hits—delivered in 0.03 seconds. Yet for all its speed and accuracy, the full potential of Internet search has yet to be reached.

Jerry Yang, appearing on PBS's *Charlie Rose* in March 2005, spoke of what he envisioned search might mean to future Web surfers. "We look at it as search is a very big space," he said. "And in fact, I think the conventional wisdom about what search is today versus where it should go and could go and will go is very different."

Today's search, he said, is relatively simple: Type in a keyword and receive results back. Those results are sometimes helpful, sometimes not, because the search application is, itself, "dumb," programmed only to match queries with relevant results. But Yang it will house will allow the best and the brightest to convene and engage in problem-solving in a unique way that's only possible in an academic setting."

Yang added, "I think in 5, 10, or 15 years, we'll be able to say, 'Wow, look at all the great things that have come out of that building.'"

Over the years at Stanford, Yang and Yamazaki have funded scholarships, undergraduate education, and other campus programs at the School of Engineering, the Asia Pacific Research Center, the Stanford Japan Center, and the Jasper Ridge Biological Preserve.

sees a brighter future for the smarter search engines with which we will interact.

"What is happening now is that search is no longer just a single-minded activity. It is going to be embedded in other activities that you do," he said. "For example, it could be part of your music experience, so if you're listening to music and you say, well, I want to find the lyric . . . or I want to know who the producer of that record is, or you're looking for a restaurant on your yellow pages online, and then you see some reviews and you say, I'd like to see what other kind of reviews this person has written.

"Search is going to get embedded into applications that people already use in other ways that they don't think of as search. So I think this idea of searching into vertical areas rather than creating vertical searches, I think people will go to a music site or go to an e-mail site or go to a content site, and then subconsciously do search.

"The other thing I think (will happen is) a lot more personalization. . . . So, you know, the search engine that I like the most ought to be able to know my habits more. So the more I use it, it's not like starting over every time. . . . The game of search has become a lot more multidimensional than any of us probably thought."

CHIEF YAHOO'S LEGACY

After Yang announced that he was stepping down as Yahoo!'s CEO, people across Silicon Valley were wondering who would replace him and what would happen to the company. Even with Yang gone, Microsoft said it was no longer interested in making another bid for Yahoo!. But, according to *The New York Times* of November 18, 2008, "Steven A. Ballmer, Microsoft's chief executive, . . . has expressed repeated interest in buying the company's search business. Many observers and Internet veterans agree that this remains the company's most attractive option."

Others believed that what Yahoo! needed was a strong leader with a clear vision who could stabilize the company and try to capitalize on its many and varied technological assets. The *Times* article reported that "the company still attracts 500 million users a month, is the leading Web e-mail service, and has other profitable Internet franchises in news, sports, and video."

One technology analyst agreed that Yahoo! would best be served by remaining intact because "(Yahoo!) isn't like AOL. They actually have a big loyal audience that isn't going away. They just need to pick their battles more sensibly."

Yang's successor, Carol Bartz, who was named CEO in January 2009, appears to be taking that advice. "I think Yahoo! has unfortunately been battered in the last year and that has caused it to look internally and be protective," Bartz told the *Times* following her appointment. "That's nonsense for such a great company and such a great franchise." Bartz had been the chief executive of Autodesk, the world's fourth-largest PC software company, for 14 years. Bartz said that after reviewing Yahoo!, she planned to turn its focus outward. She added that Yahoo! had some great assets that "frankly, could use a little management."

Despite taking the blame for the failed deal with Microsoft, Yang remains, as one Web site dubbed him, "the Internet's Jolly

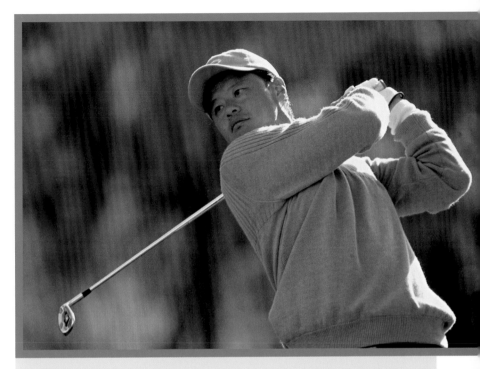

Jerry Yang hit from the 12th tee during the third round of the AT&T Pebble Beach National Pro-Am tournament held in February 2009 in California. Despite the turmoil of his tenure as CEO at Yahoo!, Yang remains the public face of one of the leading Internet companies in the world.

Grin Giant," the smiling, public face of one of the biggest Web sites on the World Wide Web. What began as a list of favorite sites compiled by two graduate students to avoid working on their theses exploded into a phenomenon that touches the lives of millions of users every single day. Thanks in part to Jerry Yang and David Filo's determination that Yahoo! remain a free site, the Web is a democratic place open to all users.

And as long as they remain behind their outdated computers, surfing the Internet alongside their legions of devoted users, the only sure thing is that *wherever* Yahoo! needs to be next, it will be somewhere out there, on the cutting edge of the World Wide Web and technology.

CHRONOLOGY

1968 Yang Chih-Yuan (Jerry Yang) is born on
November 6 in Taipei, Taiwan.
1969 The Department of Defense's ARPANET
computer network successfully links four
computers in four locations for the first time.
1970 Jerry's father dies.

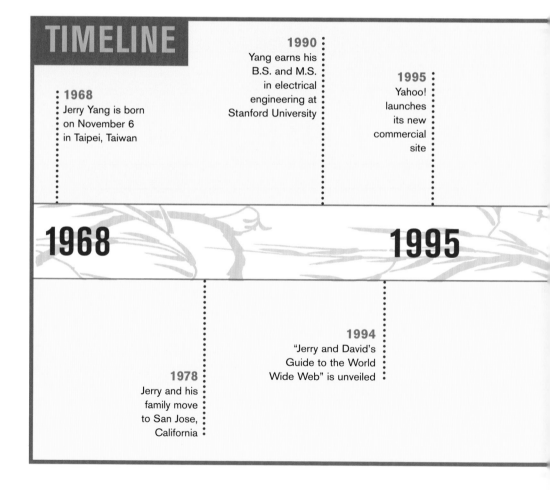

TIMELINE

1968
Jerry Yang is born
on November 6
in Taipei, Taiwan

1990
Yang earns his
B.S. and M.S.
in electrical
engineering at
Stanford University

1995
Yahoo!
launches
its new
commercial
site

1968

1995

1978
Jerry and his
family move
to San Jose,
California

1994
"Jerry and David's
Guide to the World
Wide Web" is unveiled

1978 Jerry, his mother, and his younger brother move to San Jose, California.

1990 Yang earns his B.S. and M.S. in electrical engineering at Stanford University in California, where he meets and becomes friends with another student, David Filo.

1991 Scientists at the European Laboratory for Particle Physics in Switzerland develop the World Wide Web.

1993 Marc Andreessen's Mosaic Web browser is introduced at the University of Illinois.

2000
Yahoo! stock hits a high of $237.50, then plummets as the Internet bubble bursts

2008
Microsoft makes an unsuccessful bid to buy Yahoo!

1996

2008

1996
Yahoo! goes public with its initial public offering.

2007
Yang is named CEO of Yahoo!

2008
Yang announces in November that he is resigning as CEO

1993 Yang and Filo attend a six-month program in Kyoto, Japan, cementing their friendship.

1994 Yang and Filo unveil "Jerry and David's Guide to the World Wide Web." The guide is put online in April. Soon, it is renamed Yahoo!.

1995 In August, Yahoo! launches its new commercial site, with advertisements and news feeds from Reuters. That same month, Tim Koogle is named chief executive officer of Yahoo!.

1996 With its initial public offering on April 12, Yahoo! becomes a public company with shareholders.

2000 Yahoo! stock hits a high of $237.50 a share in January. During 2000 and 2001, though, the Internet stock bubble bursts, resulting in billions of dollars of lost wealth and the closing of many companies. Yahoo! survives.

2001 Terry Semel becomes Yahoo!'s new CEO.

2005 Yahoo! faces criticism when it is revealed that a journalist was jailed after Yahoo! cooperated with Chinese authorities.

2007 Yang replaces Terry Semel as Yahoo!'s CEO in June.

2008 Microsoft makes a bid to buy Yahoo!, but Yang rebuffs the effort. In November, he announces that he will step down as CEO to resume his role as the company's Chief Yahoo.

2009 Carol Bartz is appointed as Yahoo!'s new CEO in January.

GLOSSARY

algorithm—A computer program, or series of programs, designed to systematically solve a certain kind of problem.

Archie—The first software to search and create a list of the Internet.

ARPA—The Department of Defense's Advanced Research Projects Agency, which was started in 1958. It has funded the development of technologies like computer networking.

artificial intelligence (AI)—The study and creation of intelligence in machines that is able to mimic independent human thought.

board of directors—The people elected by stockholders to set corporate policies and make management decisions.

browser—A software application used to locate and display Web pages.

chief executive officer—The highest-ranking executive in a company, responsible for carrying out the policies of the board of directors on a daily basis.

cold war—A state of political tension and military rivalry between nations that stops short of full-scale war—exemplified by what existed between the United States and the Soviet Union after World War II.

Communism—A system of government in which the state plans and controls the economy and a single, often authoritarian, party holds power, claiming to make progress toward a higher social order in which all goods are equally shared by the people.

cybernetics—The theory and science of communication and control in animals and machines.

e-commerce—Commerce conducted via the Internet.

genome—The genetic material of an organism.

Gopher—A search engine designed to search local networks.

hardware—The physical components of an apparatus, like a computer.

HTML, or HyperText Markup Language—A computer language used to create multimedia pages for the World Wide Web.

HTTP, or HyperText Transfer Protocol—A computer language commonly used on the Internet. HTTP defines how messages are formatted and transmitted and what actions Web servers and browsers should take in response to various commands.

hypertext—The computer program that allows for linking text documents to other related documents on the World Wide Web.

initial public offering (IPO)—The first time a new company offers its stock for sale to investors.

Internet—The global network of computers and other networks, including the World Wide Web.

Internet service provider (ISP)—A company that provides access to the Internet.

microprocessor—A silicon chip that contains a CPU (central processing unit), which is considered the brains of the computer.

multimedia—A combination of different means of communication, including television, radio, the Internet, and the telephone.

nationalism—A sense of national consciousness exalting one nation above all others and placing primary emphasis on the promotion of its culture and interests.

network—The connection of two or more computers by electronic means.

punch cards—Paper or cardboard cards with holes punched in them in different sequences to convey instructions to a computer or other machine.

random access—Refers to the ability to access data at random. The term is often used to describe data files.

A random-access data file enables you to read or write information anywhere in the file.

search engine—Software that categorizes and organizes Web pages into a searchable format for delivery to the user.

server—A centrally located computer that stores Web pages.

software—Computer instructions or data. Anything that can be stored electronically is software.

spider—A robotic computer program that searches the Internet by following links from site to site and recording their contents in a process known as Web crawling.

venture capitalist—An individual or a company that puts up the money to get new businesses started in exchange for part ownership.

VERONICA, or Very Easy Rodent-Oriented Network Index to Computerized Archives —An early program developed to list the contents of the Internet.

Web site—A location on the World Wide Web, usually consisting of many related pages containing text, graphics, and multimedia files.

World Wide Web—Any part of the Internet made using HTML (HyperText Markup Language).

BIBLIOGRAPHY

"2005 Annual Dinner Award Presentation: Emcee Lisa Ling's Q&A with the Honorees." Asia Society Web site, May 31, 2005. Available online. URL: http://www.asiasociety.org/support/specialevents/annual_dinner/ling_transcript.html.

"A Conversation with Jerry Yang, Cofounder of Yahoo." *Charlie Rose*, March 1, 2005. Available online. URL: http://www.accessmylibrary.com/coms2/summary_0286-3894919_ITM.

Angel, Karen. *Inside Yahoo! Reinvention and the Road Ahead.* New York: John Wiley & Sons, 2002.

Associated Press. "Yahoo Criticized in Case of Jailed Dissident." *The New York Times*, November 7, 2007. Available online. URL: http://www.nytimes.com/2007/11/07/technology/07yahoo.html?scp=1&sq=yahoo%20criticized%20in%20case%20of%20jailed%20dissident&st=cse.

Becoming American: The Chinese Experience. PBS transcript. Available online. URL: http://www.pbs.org/becomingamerican/program3_transcript.pdf.

Caplan, Jeremy. "Yahoo Goes Back to Square One." *Time*, June 1, 2007. Available online. URL: http://www.time.com/time/business/article/0,8599,1635074,00.html?xid=feed-cnn-topics.

Central Intelligence Agency. "The World Factbook: Taiwan." Available online. URL: https://www.cia.gov/library/publications/the-world-factbook/geos/tw.html.

Elgin, Ben, and Jay Greene. "The Counterattack on Google." *BusinessWeek*, May 8, 2006. Available online. URL: http://www.businessweek.com/print/magazine/content/06_19/b3983079.htm?chan=gl.

French, Howard. "China Luring Scholars to Make Universities Great." *The New York Times*, October 28, 2005. Available online. URL: http://www.nytimes.com/2005/10/28/international/asia/28universities.html?pagewanted=2&sq&st=cse%22china%20wants%20to%20transform%20its%20top%20universities%22&scp=1.

Gallagher, David, and Brad Stone. "Jerry Yang, Yahoo Chief, Plans to Step Down." *The New York Times,* November 17, 2008. Available online. URL: http://bits.blogs.nytimes. com/2008/11/17/jerry-yang-yahoo-chief-plans-to-step-down/?scp=1&sq=jerry%20yang,%20yahoo%20chief, %20plans%20to%20step%20down&st=Search.

Hamilton, Anita. "Yahoo's Next Move." *Time,* May 3, 2008. Available online. URL: http://www.time.com/time/business/ article/0,8599,1737364,00.html.

Hansell, Saul. "Yang: Microsoft Bid Was a 'Galvanizing Event' for Yahoo." *The New York Times,* February 25, 2008. Available online. URL: http://bits.blogs.nytimes.com/2008/02/25/ yang-microsoft-bid-was-a-galvanizing-event-for-yahoo/ ?scp=1&sq=microsoft%20bid%20was%20a%20galvanizing %20event&st=Search.

Helft, Miguel. "Yahoo Chief Explains Rejection of Microsoft Bid." *The New York Times,* February 14, 2008. Available online. URL: http://www.nytimes.com/2008/02/14/technology/ 14cnd-yahoo.html?scp=1&sq=yahoo%20chief%20explains %20rejection%20of%20microsoft%20bid&st=cse.

_____. "Yahoo's Chief Resigns, and a Founder Takes Over." The New York Times, June 19, 2007. Available online. URL: http://www.nytimes.com/2007/06/19/technology/ 19yahoo.html.

"The Internet's Jolly Grin Giant." Goldsea.com. Available online. URL: http://www.goldsea.com/Innovators/Yangjerry/ yangjerry.html.

"Inventor Profile: An Wang." National Inventors Hall of Fame Foundation Inc. Web site. Available online. URL: http://www. invent.org/hall_of_fame/149.html.

"Jerry Yang: The Interview." AsianConnections.com. Available online. URL: http://www.asianconnections.com/community/ people/jerry_yang/jerry_yang.php.

"Los Alamos Computer Scientist Honored as Asian American Engineer of the Year." Los Alamos National Laboratory Web site, February 13, 2004. Available online. URL: http://www. lanl.gov/news/releases/archive/04-006.shtml.

Newman, Michael. "CMU's Raj Reddy Fills Lives with Big Questions." *Pittsburgh Post-Gazette,* June 15, 1998. Available online. URL: http://www.post-gazette.com/businessnews/ 19980615braj1.asp.

Plotkin, Hal. "A Couple of Yahoos." *Metroactive*, April 11, 1996. Available online. URL: http://www.metroactive.com/papers/ metro/04.11.96/yahoo-9615.html.

Redin, James. "The Doctor and His Calculators." Available online. URL: http://www.xnumber.com/xnumber/anwang.htm.

Roessner, Jeremy. "How Yahoo! Aims to Reboot." *Time*, February 2, 2007. Available online. URL: http://www.time. com/time/magazine/article/0,9171,1584788,00.html.

Sarkar, Dibya. "Yahoo Asks U.S. Gov't to Help Dissidents." *USA Today*, February 21, 2008. Available online. URL: http://www. usatoday.com/tech/products/2008-02-21-2731094939_x.htm.

Schlender, Brent. "How a Virtuoso Plays the Web Eclectic." *Fortune*, March 6, 2000. Available online. URL: http://money. cnn.com/magazines/fortune/fortune_archive/2000/03/06/27 5253/index.htm.

Sherman, Josepha. *Jerry Yang and David Filo: Chief Yahoos of Yahoo!* Brookfield, Conn.: Twenty-First Century Books, 2001.

Shwartz, Mark. "Alumni Couple Yang and Yamazaki Pledge $75 Million to the University." *Stanford Report*, February 15, 2007. Available online. URL: http://news.stanford.edu/ news/2007/february21/donors-022107.html.

Sigismund, Charles S. *Champions of Silicon Valley: Visionary Thinking from Today's Technology Pioneers*. New York: John Wiley & Sons, 2000.

Stanford University School of Engineering Annual Report 1995–1996. "Jerry Yang and David Filo." Available online. URL: http://soe.standford.edu/about/AR95-96/jerry.html.

Stone, Brad. "Now Comes the Hard Part as Yahoo Wrestles with a Question of Direction." *The New York Times*, November 18, 2008. Available online. URL: http://www.nytimes. com/2008/11/19/technology/companies/19yahoo.html?_r=1 &scp=1&sq=%22now%20comes%20the%20hard%20part %20as%20yahoo%22&st=cse.

Stross, Randall E. "How Yahoo Won the Search Wars." *Fortune*, March 2, 1998.

"Terry Semel Biography." Encyclopedia of World Biography. Available online. URL: http://www.notablebiographies.com/news/Ow-Sh/Semel-Terry.html.

Weston, Michael R. *Jerry Yang and David Filo: The Founders of Yahoo!* New York: The Rosen Publishing Group, 2007.

"The Wired Diaries." *Wired* magazine, January 1999. Available online at http://www.wired.com/wired/archive/7.01/diaries.html.

Wu-chun Feng Home Page. Available online. URL: http://people.cs.vt.edu/~feng/.

Zia, Helen. *Asian American Dreams: The Emergence of an American People.* New York: Farrar, Straus and Giroux, 2001.

FURTHER RESOURCES

BOOKS

Filo, David and Jerry Yang, *Yahoo! Unplugged*. Foster City, Calif.: IDG Books, 1995.

Hill, Brad. *Yahoo! for Dummies*. Hoboken, N.J.: For Dummies: 2000.

Hock, Randolph. *Yahoo! to the Max: An Extreme Searcher Guide*. Medford, N.J.: Information Today, 2005.

Newquist, H.P. *Yahoo!: The Ultimate Guide to the Internet*. New York: Ibooks, 2002.

WEB SITES

Computer History Museum
http://www.computerhistory.org

Earliest Known Yahoo Web Site (From 1996)
http://web.archive.org/web/19961017235908/http://www2.yahoo.com

Yahoo!
http://www.yahoo.com

PHOTO CREDITS

INDEX

ABOUT
THE AUTHOR

PAUL KUPPERBERG is a writer and editor with more than a dozen books of nonfiction on topics including history, popular culture, science, and medicine. He has also written novels, short stories, syndicated newspaper strips, Web animation, humor and satire, as well as comic, story, and coloring books. He has been an editor on numerous national publications, including a weekly newspaper and a kids magazine. He lives in Connecticut.